Keighley Sport in Pictures

Rob Grillo

PAPERBACK EDITION ISBN: 9798333888006

HARDBACK EDITION (limited edition) ISBN: 9798333382924

All rights reserved. No part of this publication may be reproduced, stored in a retrieval system, or transmitted in any form or in any means electronic, mechanical, photograph, recording or otherwise without the permission of the copyright holders. Nor be otherwise circulated in any form or binding other than which it is published without a similar condition being imposed upon the subsequent publisher.

© **Rob Grillo 2024**

Index

	Page
Introduction	4
Sport in Keighley	6
Keighley's Sporting Heroes	9
Keighley's Sporting Arenas	30
Trading Cards & Ephemera	41
Keighley Sporting Medals & Trophies	47
Keighley & District Football Teams	53
Keighley & District Rugby Teams	113
Keighley & District Cricket Teams	138
The Runners	162
The Boxers	181
Cycling	184
Other Sports	208

Keighley Sport in Pictures

Introduction

Keighley has enjoyed a rich sporting history, with many teams and individuals making their mark. Many of those are featured in these pages. However, there are also photographs that feature others who have played for teams that were not as successful on the sporting field, but which have been just as important in shaping the culture of sport in the town.

It is impossible to include every Keighley sportsman & woman to have made their mark, or to include every team that has been successful in some way or other, but hopefully this book gives a broad coverage to a number of sports and pastimes.

Until relatively recently, women's sport has been of a much lower profile and there have been comparatively few women's football, rugby and cricket teams in existence around the Keighley district compared to men's teams, which explains why there are fewer photographs featuring ladies' sports.

Some photographs in the book were previously on display in the Vine Tavern, which is now long gone. They were scanned by Andy Wade. David Brett took many of the football photographs from around 2005 onwards.

Some of these photographs have appeared in my previous books – some of which are now out of print – but many others have not. The sources of some of the photographs are unknown, and I apologise if any copyright has been infringed or sources have not been properly acknowledged. Any mistakes will be rectified in future prints of the book. A lot of photos have come from the archives of *The Keighley News* newspaper. I was given access, thanks to the former Sports Editor Kevin Hopkinson, to their archive of photographs when researching some of my earliest books. In fact, the same newspaper has been supportive of my work right back to the early 1980s, and has continued to show the same support in recent years.

A number of images in the book may not be of the best quality. However, I've chosen to include them because they contain somebody's relative; their father, grandfather, mother, aunt or uncle for instance, and may bring memories for others. They may also be photographs of teams or individuals that really made their mark in local sporting circles, and so for that reason deserve not to be forgotten. The banner at the top of the Index page is from the long-gone *Keighley Correspondent* newspaper, 1907.

Many thanks to all those who have forwarded photographs either recently or through the years. Some of these people have helped me so many times over the past few years. In no particular order, they include: Eddie Kelly, Andy Wade. Keighley & District Local History Society, Tim Neal, The Keighley News, Eric Malcolm Binns, Helen Anstis, Philip Bland, Dave & Eileen Woodhead, Alistair Shand, Liz Spencer Petty, Thelma Norton Spencer, David Martin, Jenny Beaumont, Kirsty Ambler, Chris Melling,

Maurice Tillotson, Brian Moate, Colin Kirkham, Michelle Hughes, Margaret & Melissa Whitaker, Derek Bown, Wendy Halloway, Pete Carr, Derek Newiss, Beverley Murray, Jeff Wallbank, Kevin Hopkinson, Kirsty Ambler, Trevor Smith, David Brett, Neil & Paula Barnes, Mike Breeze, Judith Ellis, George Walker, Andy Parker, Darren Whitaker, Terry Hanson, Stephen Kennedy, Veronica Kennedy, Anne Coward, Margaret Barrett, Beth Brunskill, Lee Hamblin, Jimmy Ashworth, Barry Thomas, Shaun Neil Kelly, Andrew Winterbottom, Neil Barrett, Nick Charlesworth, Lorna Hubbard, Des Fretwell, Sheila Greenham. Eric Robshaw, Peter Moon, Steve Bainbridge, Steven Briggs, Katie Lister, Charlotte Westerman, and Chris Tordoff.

This book is dedicated to the unsung heroes who have worked behind the scenes to make sure these clubs and athletes could take part in the first place - the club secretaries, league officials, parents, family members and the like.

Grange Middle School Under 13s 1981/82 season

In order to prevent any unnecessary debate as to which has been the greatest sports team ever in Keighley then it's only fair to put that argument to rest at the beginning. Keighley's best sporting individual is open to debate, but not the best team. It's this one. Made up of several ultra-talented individuals, this team lost very few matches in its three years together at Grange. If it did lose, well that was down to either bad luck, a pure fluke, or biased refereeing. Note the legendary Grange School hall curtains in the background.

Back: Stuart Ruckledge, Jeremy Fay. Middle: Daniel Belcher, Nigel Arnold, Mark Rankin, Nigel Walker. Front: Anthony Redman, Mark Lister, Andrew Addy, Peter Dobson, Steven Briggs, Christopher Cookson. It's only fair to also mention the likes of Iain Hewitt and Taseen Amin who also played for this remarkable team. The author of this book was third choice goalie. Photo courtesy of Steve Briggs.

SPORT IN KEIGHLEY

The Factory Act of 1850 changed the climate of sport in the UK. It maintained that all work would finish at 2pm on a Saturday. This meant that for the first time the working classes could enjoy leisure time. It also marked the growth of organised sporting clubs and competitions as men began to take part in various sports. Fewer women were able to enjoy this privilege however, in most cases women's sport was seen as something of a novelty.

Sport did of course take place in the Keighley district before 1850. A traditional form of 'foot-ball' was played between local villages - Cowling and Lothersdale being examples – with a 'goal' in each village. These contests would involve dozens of local men, and there were few rules, with broken bones and bloody noses the norm.

The riotous form that such games took was referred to in Robert Holmes' *Keighley Past & Present*, who recorded that football *'was sometimes carried to a riotous and dangerous extent, township being arrayed against township and village against village'*, and that *'much excitement and alarm were often created by the great set matches between the Town and Parish of Keighley'*.

Further evidence to corroborate that foot-ball was played in this part of West Yorkshire comes from Elizabeth Gaskill's *The Life of Charlotte Bronte*, who referred to the esteemed Reverend William Grimshaw who sought to call out a religious life among his parishioners. Many of these *'had been in the habit of playing at football on Sunday, using stones for this purpose; and giving and receiving challenges from other parishes.'*

However, after Grimshaw's time, as Gaskell goes on to say, *'The games of football on Sundays, with the challenges to the neighbouring parishes, were resumed, bringing in an influx of riotous strangers to fill the public houses.'*

The law was also used to make it harder for young men to play 'foot-ball'. The Lighting, etc., of Parishes (England) Act 1830, which was 'to make provision for the lighting, watching, cleansing and paving of parishes in England and Wales', made it an offence for any person *'to fly any kite, drive any hoop, or play football or any other game or games, to the annoyance of any passenger or traveller'*.

This prevented the working classes from disrupting the business classes from going about their way, and paved the way – so to speak – for football to return to local fields and pastures from whence it came.

The Highway Act 1835 further hardened the authorities stance against the playing of football on public highways, with a maximum penalty of forty shillings for those flouting the new laws, and local by-laws allowed for the punishment of those who were caught playing foot-ball in the wrong places. In May 1905 *The Keighley News* reported that seven youths, all of Turkey and Leeds Streets had been summonsed for the terrible crime of *'playing football on the highway'* and were each fined three shillings, plus costs.

Traditionally, the playing of football had taken place off the road, however. In September 1865, valuable freehold estates were offered at Newsholme, close to Oakworth, and among several closes of land, was one named *'Foot-ball field'*. That field – thus far unlocated – will have survived to this day. It would have taken a fair effort for footballers of that time to have travelled the three miles or so from Keighley itself just for a game. (A football pitch was used in the early 1930s right in the bottom of the steep sided-Newsholme Dene. This could have been the same site as the 'foot-ball field', which could otherwise have existed higher up the hill closer to Oakworth).

A rise in Muscular Christianity played a part in the formation of specific sporting clubs in and around Keighley after the 1850 Factories Act. The local churches were able to take advantage in the rise of local sport by organising their own sports clubs and thereby increasing their own congregations. It was seen to be 'manly' and 'good in the eyes of God' to take part in sport, to show ones prowess, and so sport was encouraged. However, if you didn't go to church on the Sunday, you were not allowed to play for the team the following Saturday. Christian values were often left behind on the field of sport though, with some of the church based rugby and soccer teams becoming notorious for their foul play.

Cricket has traditionally been a middle-class pastime, and the formation of Keighley Cricket Club precedes the Factory Act by two years. Its hard to believe that Keighley's town hall square was for a short time a cricket ground before becoming a timber yard. In 1893 league cricket came to Keighley, replacing weekly friendly fixtures, with the Keighley & District, West Bradford, and West Riding Leagues housing local teams.

Keighley's professional rugby club has of course made the headlines many times over the years. The club joined the Northern Union (now of course known as Rugby League) in 1900. This was purely in order to keep a competitive fixture list as since 1895 the region's top clubs had jumped ship to the new code in order to control their own affairs rather than bow down to the London centric Rugby Football Union. The broken-time payments reason given in most rugby history books is really only part of the reason that rugby split. However, local teams Worth Village, Silsden and Sutton had actually moved over to the new code twelve months before the senior Keighley club.

The Keighley Charity Cup competition was organised in the 1889/90 season for local rugby teams in order to raise funds for the town's Victoria Hospital. However, in 1904 it was reorganised as a soccer competition, reflecting the dramatic rise of that sport.

Given Keighley's close proximity to the early soccer hotbed of East Lancashire, there was every chance that the town could have had a successful soccer team from the start, but it missed the boat in the late 1800s and by the time the game caught on in the early 1900s it was almost too late.

Soccer was less rough, and many found it easier to understand than rugby and once the game had finally taken off it had exploded in popularity by the 1920s. A Keighley & District League ran from 1905-63, and from there several teams went on to greater success. Sunday league football arrived in 1961, with the Keighley Sunday Alliance lasting until 2010. Sadly, the days when all the pitches at Marley were in use Saturday afternoons, and on both Sunday mornings and afternoons are now long gone.

The number of women taking part in mass sport was for many years very low. Women cricketers were ridiculed by the authorities. Despite that, it did briefly become popular in the 1930s and there were a number of competitions that Keighley teams could enter. In soccer the Football Association chose to ban women's football from being played on any ground under their jurisdiction from 1921. It claimed that the game was not suitable for women to play. Being a good housewife was seen as a far more important role to those that ran the game in those days.

Running as a pastime became popular in the late 1890s. Local villages and local sporting clubs would hold their summer athletics sports events on grass tracks, where there would be occasional betting on the winners. Local runners would challenge others to foot-races, although by racing on public highways those combatants would be breaking the law. Mill hands Joseph Murgatroyd and George Hartley were each fined 5s for obstructing the highway when they raced each other near Riddlesden in September 1895. Each was fined 5 shillings plus costs, but Hartley probably had the last laugh as the wager had been for the princely sum of 30 shillings.

When local athletics clubs came on the scene (the first club in Keighley was in 1893), runners were not always popular even when they ran off the road. In those days club runs consisted of paper chases, whereby a couple of runners – 'hares' - would set off first, laying a paper trail as they did so. The main 'pack' would follow some time later. The pack would stick together until one designated member cracked a whip about a mile from home, and everyone then raced back to where they had started. The laying of paper was not exactly popular among some, and local farmers often had to rebuild walls and close gates after a pack had charged through their land.

Women's athletics became more popular in the 1920s and in 1933 the first Yorkshire and Bradford cross country championships were held for women, over courses of around three miles. It was still thought by then that long distance running would harm women (and well into the 1980s those same ideas prevailed among those in authority), and local road races in the main excluded women until the 1970s.

Keighley Golf Club was founded on 7th February 1904, following a meeting of members of Keighley Skating Club at the old Mechanics Institute on North Street. Discussions to set up the club had begun the previous year. The ice skaters had felt restricted by the indoor roller skating rinks which were popular at the time, and wanted an outdoor activity to see them through the summer months.

A proposal to utilise land around Tarn House during the summer months was passed. As a result, a nine-hole course was marked out on land above Tower House on the heights above Utley. In 1908 a move was made to its present location, initially renting Howden Park (part of an old historic deer park) from Lord Hothfield. Despite its current ageing membership, Keighley Golf Club has continued to serve the town since then.

Migrants to Keighley have played a massive part in shaping sport in Keighley. The Irish communities, who arrived initially in the 1840s were not initially popular. Refugees from the awful potato famines there, many such migrants were very poor and lived in their own communities in areas such as High Utley. As they became established they founded their own sporting clubs, the Shamrock club at the bottom of West Lane being one of the more prominent – the name of Keighley Shamrocks is especially well known in the world of rugby and football.

In more recent times, migrants from South Asia have helped to keep other sports clubs going. Local cricket , for example, is indebted to those from the likes of India, Pakistan and Bangladesh . Sports teams representing Italian and East European communities have also made their mark locally.

Saturday 14th July 1956 proved an important occasion for Keighley sport, with the opening of the new athletics track and sporting complex at Marley. Much of the town's sporting history has been centred on this fantastic sporting facility, and even though the track is long gone (there's now a much better one up Greenhead Road of course) it remains a sporting hub to this day.

In recent years, the number of soccer (in particular), rugby and cricket teams in the town has fallen, reflecting a nationwide trend. Silsden and Riddlesden Golf Clubs have been forced to close, as have clubs and local competitions in many other sports. Running and cycling are still very popular, and there are still plenty of individuals either excelling in their chosen sports, and taking the time to organise and encourage others in their endeavours.

KEIGHLEY'S SPORTING HEROES

Harry Myers

Born in 1875, Harry Myers originally played for his home-town club, Horsforth. He came to Keighley in 1896, remaining with the club when it joined the Northern Union (now Rugby League) in 1900. He was capped once by England playing in the 6–9 defeat by Ireland at the Athletic Ground, Richmond, London on Saturday 5th February 1898.

On 3rd November 1906 Myers was knocked unconscious in an accidental collision while playing for Keighley at Dewsbury. Despite regaining consciousness he died on the evening of 19th December. His funeral was held four days later. The funeral procession marched from the Worth Valley Hotel at Ingrow, where he was the licensee, to Keighley Parish Church. He was buried in Utley cemetery and it was estimated that over 10,000 people lined the route of the procession (photograph below). He left a wife, Ada, and four children.

Terry Hollindrake

Probably Keighley's greatest Rugby League player, Terry Hollindrake (1934-2015) was a product of Keighley Albion. He went on to become the only Keighley-born full internationally capped Rugby League player when he featured for Great Britain in the Third Test at Headingley against New Zealand on 17th December 1955.

He signed for Keighley in December 1951, making his debut against Salford in January 1953. Following a period of National Service, he continued to play for the club, scoring a record 26 tries during the 1955/56 season. He beat that two seasons later, with a total of 27 tries. Hollindrake also represented Yorkshire five times during the 1958/59 season.

He moved to Hull in 1960, scoring 206 points in 114 matches for them, before moving to Bramley in 1964 where he scored 604 points in 144 games. Hollindrake left Bramley in 1968 and played a single season for Keighley Shamrocks, before re-signing to Keighley for the 1969/70 season where he played a further 26 games scoring 9 tries and 4 goals before retiring in 1970. In all he, scored 236 tries and 546 goals as a professional player, giving a grand total of 1800 points.

Saima Hussain

In 2006 Saima Hussain, who at the time played Rugby League for the Keighley Cats walked away with the award for the Most Up & Coming Sports Personality of the Year in the Sony Entertainment Sports Personality Awards.

Saima, a sports development officer, was at the time the only Asian female rugby league player in the country, and was the first Muslim female to play Rugby League for Yorkshire and Great Britain.

She has gone on to further help promote the sport among ethnic communities and continues to be a important ambassador for the game.

Danny Jones

Danny Jones will forever be remembered when he died whilst playing for Keighley Cougars in 2015.

Born in Halifax, on 6th March 1986, Jones played for amateur teams, Ovenden and King Cross before turning professional with Halifax, making his first team début as a 17-year-old. He remained with Halifax until 2006 when he joined Keighley for the start of the 2007 season. After four seasons with Keighley, he returned to Halifax for the 2011 season but then moved back to Keighley in 2012.

Playing as a stand-off or scrum-half, Jones made his international debut in 2010, a defeat by Italy, and was named in the Wales squad for the 2013 Rugby League World Cup.

During a League One match between Keighley Cougars and London Skolars on 3rd May 2015, Jones was substituted after only four minutes after feeling unwell. Soon after he went into cardiac arrest, and received treatment at the scene. Transferred by air ambulance to the Royal Free hospital, he later died. The match was abandoned and a post-mortem revealed that the cardiac arrest was caused by a previous undetected, hereditary, heart disease.

Cougars later announced that the number 6 shirt number worn by Jones during the 2015 season would be retired with immediate effect, and the main stand at Cougar Park was named The Danny Jones Stand.

Jones' widow, Lizzie, performed the traditional Challenge Cup Final hymn, *Abide With Me* before the 2015 Challenge Cup Final, to thank players, fans and officials for their support. She also sang *Danny Boy* at the BBC Sports Personality of the Year awards in December 2015.

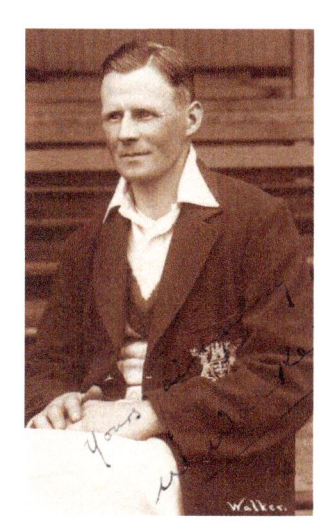

Willis Walker

Born in Gosforth, Northumberland, Walker lived in Keighley, and also played cricket for Notts in the County Championship. He played soccer as a goalkeeper for South Shields, Bradford Park Avenue, Leeds City, and Stockport County. County acquired him for £800 in an auction in 1919 after the Leeds City club was thrown out of the Football League for illegal wartime payments. His name is familiar with local sportsmen in the name of the former Keighley sports shop on Cavendish Street that he founded in 1921, not long after moving to the town. He died at home in East Morton, aged 99, in 1991.

Mike Hellawell

Born in 1938, Mike became the first Keighley born player to represent England. His Football League debut was made on 25th February 1956 for Queens Park Rangers as an outside left in a Third Division (South) fixture against Exeter City. He later went on to play for Birmingham City, Sunderland, and Huddersfield Town among others. It was with Birmingham that he really made his mark, appearing twice as an outside right for Walter Winterbottom's England side in October 1962 (At Hillsborough v France & in Belfast against Northern Ireland), winning a League Cup winners medal in 1963, and gaining experience in the European Fairs Cup competition two years before that.

Before hanging up his boots, Mike was player coach with Crosshills during the 1970's, and then turned to referring the game in the local area. As a cricketer, he played for Yorkshire's Second and Colts teams, and also captained Keighley Cricket Club in the early 1970's. While at Birmingham City he also spent two years cricketing with Warwickshire CCC. Ever popular, he passed away in 2023, less than three years after having written his autobiography.

Trevor Hockey

Trevor remains one of Keighley's best known and flamboyant sports stars. The Welsh international made his Football League debut as a 16-year-old for Bradford City against Shrewsbury Town in April 1960. He moved to Nottingham Forest in November 1961, before going on to Newcastle United (winning a Second Division championship medal in 1965), Birmingham City (where he had his own fan club and recorded a 'pop' single), Sheffield United, Norwich City and Aston Villa, before returning to Bradford City for two seasons during the mid 1970s, securing nine Welsh caps in the process. His first was at Swansea against Finland in October 1971 and his last almost two years later in Poland. He also managed Athlone Town (as player-manager) and Stalybridge Celtic and sampled the game as player-manager in the North American Football League for sides such as San Jose Earthquakes and Los Angeles Quicksilvers before returning to Keighley to play locally. Hockey revived Keighley Town AFC in 1979, and his soccer camps brought enjoyment to hundreds of schoolchildren (and their parents). His sudden death in 1987, aged just 43, was much lamented,

Maurice Lindley

Another of Keighley's sons to sample life in the Football League, as a player and then in management, Maurice Lindley began his career with Ingrow United in the Keighley League and then at Barnoldswick Town. After a couple of 'A' team games for Bradford City he signed for Everton in 1936, playing as wing half or centre half.

He stayed at Goodison Park until 1951, when he left to become coach at Swindon Town, taking over as manager two years later. Lindley left there in April 1955 before a short spell in charge at Barry Town, and then two years at Crewe. He later joined Leeds United as chief scout, and then, during the 1965-66 season became assistant to manager Don Revie. He also spent several brief periods as caretaker manager there.

His highly successful era there ended in 1982. Roy McFarlane, the manager at Bradford City then took him on a chief scout. He was rightly rewarded with a testimonial when Bradford City and Leeds United met at Valley Parade in a curtain raiser for the 1991/92 season. He died in 1994, aged 78.

Jeff Hall

Although Jeff Hall hailed from Scunthorpe and lived just outside Keighley, in Wilsden, his links with the town are such that he deserves inclusion

In his early years, Jeff played for his village team, as well as Keighley St Anne's, before signing for Bradford Park Avenue at the age of 18. Signed by Birmingham City he made his debut for them at the age of 20 against Bury in January 1951, going on to make 254 appearances for them and playing in the 1956 FA Cup final. He also appeared 17 times for his country, featuring in England's first ever international against Brazil in 1956, and only once appeared in a losing side for his country. While still in his prime, Jeff was cruelly struck down with polio, only months after marrying, passing away on 4th April 1959 aged just 29. For many years, teams in Keighley's Sunday League competed for the Jeff Hall Trophy, which was a league cup competition.

Peter Jackson

First making his name as captain of a strong Keighley schoolboy's team in the 1970's, Peter Jackson first signed schoolboy terms with Burnley before being offered an apprenticeship with Bradford City in July 1977. His debut for the Bantams came on 1st April 1979 against Torquay United, and by the 1984/85 season he had become club captain, holding that role during the traumatic period that followed the tragic Bradford City fire.

After playing nearly 300 times for City, there followed a move into the top flight with Newcastle United in October 1986, for what then equalled the Magpies record transfer payment of £250,000. He was voted player of the year in his first season there. After 60 games with them, he returned to Bradford City, playing 58 times before his departure to Huddersfield Town in 1990. After 155 appearances there, he signed for Chester City in 1994.

Peter began the 1997/98 season playing for Halifax Town, but jumped at the chance of becoming manager back at Huddersfield. After having guided the side to 10th place in Division One he was controversially sacked in 1999 to make way for Steve Bruce.

He was reappointed as manager at Leeds Road in 2003, guiding the side to promotion back to Division Two via the play-offs. In March 2007 however he had left again. Between October of that year and September 2009 he was manager at Lincoln City, winning the 'League Manager of the Month' Award.

During this time, early in 2008, Jackson was diagnosed with throat cancer. In June of the same year he was told that treatment had been successful.

Jackson became Bradford City manager in February 2011, initially on an interim basis. That summer he was given the role on a one-year basis, but after a poor start he resigned.

Right: Peter Jackson is seated third from right in this photograph of the successful Greenhead School team, taken in the mid 1970s.

Lee Duxbury

First noticed while playing for Sutton Juniors, Lee Duxbury became a favourite at Valley Parade, playing over 270 games in two spells there, scoring 32 times in the process. His debut came in 1988, and his stay at Bradford lasted until 1994 when he signed for Huddersfield Town (there was also a short loan spell at Rochdale). The following year Duxbury re-signed for City, as captain, before leaving again in 1997 for £350,000, for Oldham Athletic. At Boundary Park he again he proved a massive success as captain, playing nearly 250 times, scoring 32 times. His Football League career finished at Bury before short spells at the likes of Harrogate Town, Farsley Celtic and Glenavon.

He later became first team coach and reserve team manager at Oldham, as well as manager at Eccleshill United.

Geoff Smith

Goalkeeper Geoff Smith had also made a name for himself in the colours of Bradford City. In the 1957/58 season he established a joint club record of 18 clean sheets, helping the club to third place in the Third Division (North). The Bradford City team photograph opposite, which features Smith, is from the 1955/56 season.

Discovered by City while playing for the successful Central Youth Club junior side in 1948, he was initially released before being invited back for a trial following a spell playing for Nelson and Rossendale United. His debut came on 17th January 1953, and despite conceding four goals at Scunthorpe United that day, kept his place in the team. He played 200 consecutive games for City between 28th April 1954 and 11th October 1958, a run of four seasons ever-present. In all he played 270 times for the club.

Maurice Tillotson

Maurice Tillotson is a great example of a local lad made good after moving abroad. Following trials at Leeds United and Huddersfield Town, the Silsden footballer signed as a professional with the latter, at the age of seventeen. He had trials for the England Youth team, and went on to play in the Football League with Stockport County, with a short spell with Toronto FC in the Canadian Soccer League.

He then made more than one hundred appearances for Royal Antwerp FC of Belgium and featured in several European Cup games for that club. After moving to New Zealand he played three seasons for Gisborne City FC in the National League, where he gained selection for his adopted country and was voted NZ Player of the year in 1973. Tillotson was later appointed Player/Coach of National League team Stop Out FC where he gained further NZ International appearances.

Having retired from playing, he went into coaching in New Zealand and worked in the role of Technical Director for the Cook Islands FA for four years (Photo courtesy of Maurice himself).

Ellie Kildunne

England international Ellie is still enjoying her highly successful career in the world of Rugby Union. After starting out playing Rugby League for Keighley Albion and Union for Keighley RUFC she moved to West Park (Leeds) and then Castleford. In 2021 she signed for Harlequins, who play in the Women's Premiership, after a season with Gloucester-Hartpury.

Kildunne's England career commenced in 2017, scoring a try in her debut against Canada. Since then she has played in the 2021 World Cup in New Zealand (actually held in 2022 due to Covid), the 2020 and 2024 Olympics in Rugby 7's, and has appeared regularly in the Women's Six Nations championship. She finished as leading try scorer in 2024 Six Nations (Photo by Stefano Delfrate).

Brenda Atkinson

Atkinson is a multiple British track and road race champion, winning four British National Individual Sprint Championships in the space of five years (1978, 1979, 1980 & 1982) and three road race titles in 1978, 1979 and 1982. She was also the first woman to ride the Three Peaks Cyclo-Cross event.

Harry Binns

Erroneously referred to as J B Carr in an earlier book, Binns was one of Keighley's first crack runners. Here he is with his haul of trophies in the early years of the 20th Century.

Colin Kirkham

Colin, who moved to Coventry after having grown up in Keighley, competed in the 1972 Olympic Marathon in Munich where he finished inside the top 20. A year earlier he had finished fourth in the European Games Marathon. He also won the famous Greek Marathon over the original Olympic course, as well as others in Bermuda, Israel, the Netherlands and southern Germany. He still lives in Coventry (Photo courtesy of Colin himself).

Steve Binns

One of Keighley's most popular sporting sons, Steve earned a worldwide reputation with his performances throughout the late 1870s and '80s. A product of Oakbank School and Bingley Harriers, he broke the World Junior 5,000m record in September 1979 at Crystal Palace with a time of 13 minutes 27.1 seconds, defeating the Olympic Champion Lasse Viren at the same time. Earlier in the year he had lifted the European junior title in Poland.

After a short spell in the USA, Steve stepped up to the 10,000 metres, winning the AAA title in 1983, earning him his first appearance at the World Athletics Championships. Four years later he achieved fifth place in the World Championship in Italy over that distance in a famous race where the timekeepers rang the bell signalling the last lap one lap early.

However, what was perhaps Steve's most newsworthy performance came in the 1986 Commonweath Games 10,000, in Edinburgh. He lead the race right from the start, dropping the opposition one-by-one only to be overtaken in the final straight by team-mate Jon Solly, who had defeated him in the AAA championship earlier in the year.

Another AAA title followed in 1988, as well as Olympic Games selection before injury and illness got the better of him. In 1990 he moved with his wife Diane to Lockerbie in Scotland, but in more recent times has resided in East Yorkshire.

Steve also won a number of domestic cross country titles, finishing second in the World Junior championships in 1979. He also competed at that level as a Senior, and ran a brisk 2 hour 13 minute marathon in Chicago in 1988.

Left: Steve Binns (right) & team-mate Colin Moore at the National Cross Country Championship in Luton in 1979. Binns led from start to finish that day, finishing nearly half a minute clear of his nearest rival. Moore finished sixth.

Colin Moore

Colin Moore, a school and club mate of Steve Binns, represented Britain over 10,000 metres in the 1990 European Championships in Yugoslavia. By then he was a well established distance runner who had won his first Yorkshire Cross Country title in his first year as Senior in 1982, after having already represented his country in the World Junior Cross Country Championships in Limerick in 1979. He later set what was then a UK all-comers record over the Half Marathon distance when he won the 1985 Gateshead Half marathon in 62 minutes 22 seconds. Victory in the 1994 Houston Marathon earned selection for that years' Commonwealth Games in Edmonton, where he finished in eighth place. He enjoyed numerous other Yorkshire and Inter- Counties titles (Photo by Eric North, courtesy of Peter Moon).

Steve Brooks

Pictured with the National Junior Cross Country trophy, which he won in 1989, Steve is a former Greenhead pupil, winning his first Bradford Schools' title in 1983. Three years later he was in the England Schools team. Following a stint at Iowa University, Steve earned selection for the England Junior team at the World Cross Country Championship in New Zealand, where he finished 57th. His victory in the National Championship in 1989 saw him defeat the red hot favourites John Dennis (Camberley) and Darren Mead (Thetford), and that earned him another World Championship appearance in Stavanger, Norway. Further international honours in the Senior ranks followed on the Fells (going to the World Championship with team-mate Andy Peace), on the track, and over the country, with a further World Championship appearance.

A stunning 2.13.55 marathon at London earned Steve selection for the 1997 Athens World Championship - this after a remarkable 61 minutes 28 second half marathon in The Hague, having moved to the Netherlands. Sadly, back problems meant that he was unable to take his place on the starting line in the Greek capital.

Kim McDonald

First coming to prominence as a 14-year-old in 1971, and spending some time at Western Kentucky University Kim won a whole load of track titles at 5,000 metres before stepping up to the marathon. He was also a non-travelling reserve for England's junior team at the World Cross Country Championship.

However, he was not lost to the sport when he hung up his spikes, founding Kim McDonald International management (KIM) in order to represent international athletes in their efforts to get into races and maximise their potential financially. Based in Teddington, London, he went on to represent the likes of Steve Ovett, John Walker, Peter Elliot, Sonia O'Sullivan as well as a whole host of Kenyan distance runners. His charges broke numerous World Records and won a whole host of Olympic and World records.

He died suddenly in November 2001, his passing mourned by the worldwide athletics community, particularly from those in Kenya.

Jimmy Ashworth

The former Bingley Harrier and one time 'flying bin man', Jimmy is the fastest middle and long distance runner ever to wear a Keighley vest.

Photographed opposite en-route to victory in the Barnsley Half Marathon, Jimmy came to prominence in 1983 when winning the Manchester Piccadilly Marathon, as well as finishing runner-up in the Berlin Marathon. He went on to finish seventh in the London Marathon in 1984 and in 1985 won the Berlin event in 2 hours 11.14, as well as taking first place in the Orange Bowl Marathon in Miami earlier that year. In 1986 he was the first British runner to finish in the New York Marathon but missed out on selection for that years' Commonwealth Games.

Switching to Keighley Road Runners early in 1987, he continued to make a mark before injury and illness curtailed his time at the top. He later moved to Todmorden Harriers having opened a café there. He still coaches runners to this day (Photo courtesy of Jimmy himself).

Catherine Bennett

Catherine came to prominence in the colours of Keighley Athletic Club in 1980s as she became a consistently successful cross country runner on the regional and national stage. By 1982 the Oakbank Student was running in the colours of Bingley Harriers, already having gained medals of various colours at county and Northern championship levels in her age-group. The 1982/83 season saw her sweep all before her, with victories in the Yorkshire, West Yorkshire Schools, Northern, Inter Counties and National Cross Country championships. She also finished runner-up in the English Schools Championship (and in the ensuing Schools International race) despite being a year younger than many of her rivals. This earned her a 'Young Athlete of the Month' award by the Daily Mail (She is photographed receiving her prize from Olympian Alan Pascoe).

Twelve months later the teenager, coached by John Waterhouse did win that English Schools title. She also achieved success on the track at this level, and if you look carefully, her picture is in Dame Kelly Holmes' autobiography.

Ian Holmes

Ian first came to prominence in the early 1990s with a number of victories in classic Fell Running events, and gaining international recognition in 1992. In 1996 he became English and British Fell Running champion, also winning the Three Peaks race in 1997, a full eight minutes clear of his nearest rival. He became a regular in the England team, appearing in the World championships on several occasions.

However, Ian is perhaps best known for his three consecutive victories between 1997-99 in the Mount Kinabalu Race in Borneo, Indonesia. The race entails a five and a half mile climb to the summit at over 7,500 feet, followed by a perilous descent, which happens to be one of Ian's strengths.

The photograph to the left, courtesy of David & Eileen Woodhead, shows Ian on his way to victory in the 2006 Stanbury Splash.

Andy Peace

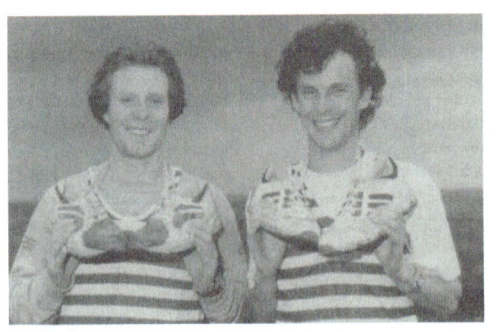

Yet another Oakbank student, Andy formed part of a crack second generation of runners from the school that included his twin brother Martin (who is on the right in the photograph) and Shaun Winstanley. A talented all-round sportsman, he decided to concentrate on Fell Running in the late 1980s, with considerable success. He arrived on the International stage with a 8th place finish in the Junior Men's race in the 1987 World Mountain Running Championship in Switzerland. Two years later he was in the England Senior team for the same championships in France. His best position on the world stage as a senior was an impressive 9th place in 1996.

Back home, Andy's list of victories in significant events is substantial, his three successive victories in the gruelling 24-mile Three Peaks race between 1994-96 being a highlight, the third of which he won in a record time of 2 hours 46 minutes (he won it again in 2004). He also became the first person to win that race and the Three Peaks Cycle Cross event in the same year, when in 1995 he rode to victory over the same three mountains, a feat he repeated twelve months later.

On top of that, Andy also competed in Duathlon events, winning the National title in 1996 (he was runner up twelve months later), and finishing ninth in that event in the World Championships in Spain in 1997.

As if that wasn't enough, Andy later finished in the top 10 in the World Ultra Running Championship, making him one of the few people ever to finish in the top 10 in the World Championship in three different disciplines. A contender for Keighley's greatest ever sportsman perhaps?

Opposite: Ian Holmes chases Andy Peace up Pendle Hill, and below a young Jonny Brownlee, Olympic Triathlon medallist, chases Andy at the Auld Lang Syne race above Top Withins (Both photographs courtesy of Dave & Eileen Woodhead).

Ambreen Sadiq

The first Asian Muslim female to box in the UK, Ambreen made national headlines in January 2010 when she was featured on a Channel 4 Documentary. The previous year, at the age of 15, she had become an ABA National Champion but had divided opinion within her community as to whether she should continue to take part in her sport. Alongside Ambreen in the documentary were several of her supportive school-friends from Belle Vue Girls School in Bradford. Now in her thirties, and the mother of two children, she is a boxing coach, and also a personal trainer.

In February 2010, Ambreen was short-listed for a British Asian Sports Award in the Junior Female Sports Personality of the Year category at a ceremony held at Grosvenor House Hotel, London. She had certainly come a long way since taking up Boxing three years earlier when she accompanied her brother to a boxing club at Eastburn, close to her home in Keighley.

Percy Vear

Hermann 'Percy' Vear, a well known professional boxer (12th July 1911 – 16th March 1983), hailed from Crossflatts, but was a resident of Keighley throughout his adult life. His boxing name is a play on the word 'Persevere'

He was one of the most colourful characters in local professional boxing scene in the 1920s and 1930s. and was managed by Keighley boxing promoter Sam Scaife

In an era when 30 fights per year was not uncommon, Percy fought initially as a flyweight, before moving to the bantamweight then featherweight divisions. In all he had 131 bouts between February 1929 and November 1934, his first as a 17-year-old.

Following his boxing career, Vear was the fitness and exercise coach at Keighley Town FC during the club's brief stint in the Yorkshire League after World War Two.

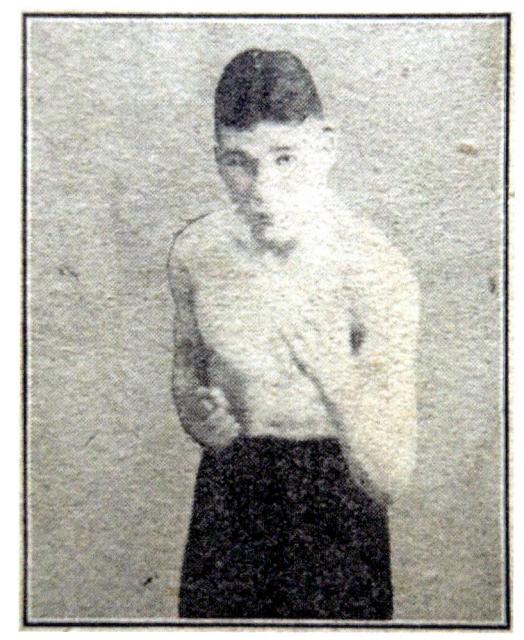

After passing away in 1983 his name again lives on as his grandson is licensee of the Aireworth Street pub 'Percy Vear's'

Chris Melling

Chris Melling has made a considerable mark in the world of professional pool and snooker, where he has excelled in all professional variations. He won the World Eightball Championship twice, in 2001 and 2003 and was ranked number one in the World in 2003 by the World Eightball Pool Federation.

Melling has also won the International Pool Masters championship in 2001 and 2002 and the European Professional title in 2002, as well as competing professionally on the Snooker circuit (he has achieved 29 x 147 breaks by June 2024). He has a whole of host of championship wins around the world. By 2014 he had become the first person to have been a professional in 8-Ball Pool, 9-Ball Pool and Snooker at the same time. Still competing to this day, Melling's walk-on music is from the song 'A Kind of Magic' by Queen (Photo courtesy of Chris himself).

Rebecca Kenna

Rebecca Kenna (née Granger) is a former Greenhead student who initially made a mark locally playing football. However, after taking up snooker seriously she has risen to the top of the sport.

She competes on the World Women's Snooker Tour, as well as the Professional World Snooker Tour where she competes against the men.

Kenna started playing on the women's snooker circuit in 2016, and reached the semi-finals of the World Championship at her first attempt. She ended her first full season ranked sixth, having reached the semi-finals of the World Championship again.

In 2018, she reached the final of the World Women's Billiards Championship, before losing to the multi-award winner Emma Bonney.

Kenna was one of four players selected to take part in the Women's Tour Championship 2019, to be held at the Crucible Theatre in August of that year. She is now the co-owner of Cue Sports Yorkshire, which sells cues and accessories, and works as a snooker coach.

Peter Judson

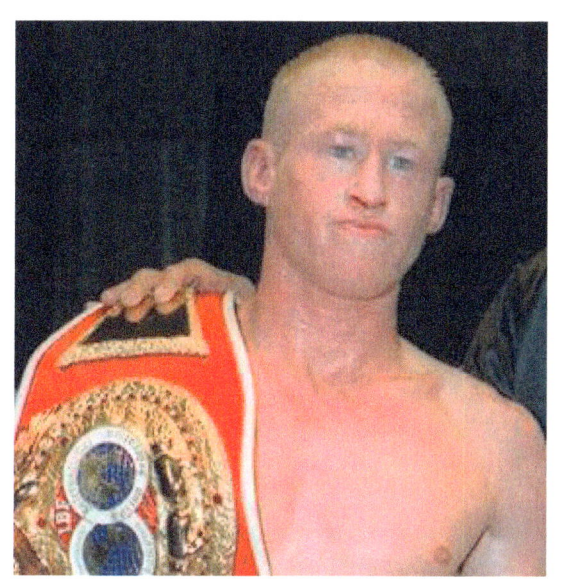

Another former Greenhead student who made their mark in the world of sport is boxer Peter Judson. Undefeated between 1982 and 1985, during that time he fought for the vacant IBF Inter-continental Super Featherweight title against Dean Phillips, wearing down the Welshman to win in ten rounds.

Nicknamed *The Bulldog*, as a tribute to the remarkable spirit he showed in fights, Judson also fought unsuccessfully for British titles and became a regular on championship promotions before retiring from the sport in his 30s.

Gary Felvus, in the 1980s, and the likes of Freddie Irving, Johnny Barratt, Arthur Barnes, Hal Bairstow and Jonny Sedgwick in the 1930s are other local boxers who have made their mark over the years. (Photo from Peter Judson twitter)

Dr John Purcell

Dr. John Purcell arrived in Silsden in 1880, from the village of Feakle in County Clare, to join a small doctor's surgery in St John Street. He was a larger than life character who was instrumental in the founding of several sports clubs sports into the community, and for over 40 years, visited his patients on horseback.

He founded Silsden AFC in 1904 (the club originally intended to be called Silsden Clarence). Keen to encourage Cobbydalers to improve their health by being actively involved in sports, he also started the town's handball and rugby clubs in the late 1890's.

He arranged a 21 year lease agreement for the current Keighley Road sports ground with the then landlords, The Skipton Castle Estate. In 1921 ground was then bought by Silsden Sports Club for £500

Purcell remained in Silsden until his death in 1927. His descendents still live in Feakle.

David Humphreys

Early in 1951 Riddlesden's David Humphreys, then 16, joined Bingley Harriers. During his seven year running career he became the club's first senior international. As a youth he won the Halifax, Bradford and Yorkshire Cross Country titles and was 4th in the National championship. He won the prestigious Burnsall fell race three years in succession in 1955, 1956 and 1957, breaking the record twice. In 1957, as a senior and having finished 10th in the nine-mile National, he was selected to run for England in the International Cross County Championship (now known as the World Championship) where he was the country's sixth counter in 39th position. He was forced to retire in 1958 due to a kidney problem. Humphrey's is seen in the centre of the photograph. To his immediate left is Derrick Lawson, World Veterans champion over 25K in 1985.

Doug Petty

Doug Petty (1930-2022) was a successful professional cyclist who made a mark even after he retired from professional racing.

He formed Keighley Velo Cycling Club in 1947 in his mum and dad's house, turned professional in 1953 and later went on to form the Croad Automatic cycling team in 1965 until 1970 when he retired from the pro ranks.

He also instigated a warm weather training camp in Majorca in 1968, and in 2003 was presented with an award for his part in helping tourism on the island.

Doug also promoted races in Victoria Park, as part of the Keighley Festival of cycling in the 1960's (Photos courtesy of Liz Spencer Petty, Doug's wife).

Des Fretwell

Born in July 1955, Silsden's Des Fretwell took up cycling aged 15, enjoying club runs with Keighley Road Club. After that he went on to ride in France for the Velo Club de Roubaix for two seasons, as well as the Cutty Sark sponsored Archer Road Club in London. He was then invited to join the all-conquering Manchester Wheelers sponsored club team which dominated British racing in the 1970/80's.

Following over 30 wins in the junior ranks, Des earned selection for the GB junior team for the European Champs on both road and track, before going on to achieve over 120 career wins as a senior.

Selection for the England team in the 1978 Commonwealth Games in Edmonton, Canada followed, with a seventh place finish in the individual road race. After winning two of the trial races, Des was then selected for the 1980 Moscow Olympics, as a member of the Great Britain team that defied mechanical problems (as well as a British Prime minister who suggested that GB should boycott the games) to finish ninth in the 100 kilometre team time trial.

Among his other feats, Des was a national track champion, and a medal winner in two disciplines despite there being no tracks in the Keighley area to train or race on. He represented GB around 200 times in total.

Best known as a fast finisher at the end of long road races, Des also finished third in the British Road Championship in 1978 behind Robert Millar and was winner of the Langollen to Wolverhampton race the same year. This was a one-off event to celebrate the anniversary of the first official road race on British roads. There were many other International race wins at home and abroad, and was the first person to win the Girvan International 3 day race twice, achieving a record number of stage wins there.

Sadly a recurrent leg injury forced Keighley's finest cyclist to retire while at his peak, but Des still cycles socially and was a pretty decent runner in the 1980s with Keighley Road Runners.

The photo above shows Des outsprinting Steve Wakefield to win the 1979 VAT Watkins GP event. The bottom photo (taken by Werner Moller) shows Des with Bob Downs, Sandy Gilchrist and Robert Millar at the 1978 World Championship Team Time Trial.

David & Eileen Woodhead

In 2015 David and Eileen Woodhead were awarded MBE's for their services to running through the years. After having been competitive runners during the late 70s and early 80s, the popular couple first organised the Stanbury Splash Fell Race in 1984, going on to introduce other races around Haworth; the Heathcliffe & Cathy Canter in 1989, the Oxenhope 'Stoop' race in 1990, the Withins Skyline in 1992, and Auld Lang Syne in 1994. Easter Bunny Runs were first organised on Harden Moor from 1992 before relocating them to Penistone Hill Country Park at Haworth. A few other one-off races have also been and gone. Their races have always been incredibly well attended, and enjoyed (**) by international runners, Olympians, and causal runners alike.

In 2017 the couple decided to step back from race organisation (Wharfedale Harriers now organise many of these races) and since then have concentrated on photographing runners around Gods Own Country and beyond. They still organise the Yorkshire Fell Senior and Junior championships and are the Yorkshire Fell Senior and Junior Inter County team selectors.

Said to be 'Chuffed' about gaining their awards David and Eileen passion for the sport of fell running remains unwavering to this day.

(Photos courtesy of the Woodentops)

(**) even the boggy ones in freezing cold conditions

Brian Sellers

One of Yorkshire Cricket's all-time greats, Brian Sellers was born in Keighley in 1907 and went on to lead the county to a unique six county championships in eight seasons before the Second World War. In all he played 334 first class matches for Yorkshire between 1932-48, most of them as captain, before becoming a prominent committee member at Headingley.

After leading Yorkshire to the Championship title for three consecutive years to 1939, Sellers was named as a Wisden Cricketer of the Year in the 1940 edition of the famous Almanack. He remained an amateur throughout his remarkable career.

Sellers was also an England Test team selector between 1938–55. He died in February 1981, at Eldwick, aged 73

Dougie Lampkin

Hailing from Silsden, Dougie earned world status in professional motorcycle trials and endurocross events. He won the motorcycle trials world outdoor championship seven times in succession between 1997-2003, as well winning the Indoor Championship five times and British title on six occasions. The Scottish six days trial has also been won 14 times, as well as two Spanish titles and four World Team Championships. Overall he is the second most successful trials rider in history, with 34 titles to his name

Dougie wasn't the first in his family to be successful in the sport. His father, Martin, was the first FIM Trial World Championship winner in 1975, and his Uncle, Arthur Lampkin, was also a regular winner on the British circuit in the 1960s.

In the 2002 New Year Honours, he was awarded the MBE for services to Motorcycle Trials Riding. He now lives on the Isle of Man.

KEIGHLEY'S SPORTING ARENAS

Lawkholme Lane

'Keighley Rugby and Association Football Club' was founded on 17th October 1876 and managed to secure a field owned by E Holmes on Lawkholme Lane. One month later, the first game took place there against Crosshills. The game ended in a draw. It is unclear whether this is the same site as the current ground. The club soon moved to a better ground on Dalton Lane.

However, Keighley Athletic Club was founded in 1879, securing use of a field on Lawkholme Lane adjacent to the cricket ground before merging with the above 'Rugby and Association Football Club' at Dalton Lane.

However, when the cricket club decided to start up its own football club in April 1885, an agreement was made for a further merger with the Dalton Lane based club instead, which meant that rugby returned to Lawkholme Lane. The rest, they say, is history.

The first two photographs, both probably taken before World War One illustrate the open nature of the ground, and the narrow border between it and the adjacent cricket pitch.

CRICKET AND FOOTBALL GROUND, KEIGHLEY.

By the time the photograph below was taken in 1938, the stadium had been developed to include its imposing main stand.

Lawkholme Lane around 1905

These are some of the ten photographs taken by photography company Hall & Siggers in the early years of the 20th Century. It is believed that Harry Myers played in this match for the Keighley club, who are playing in white jerseys.

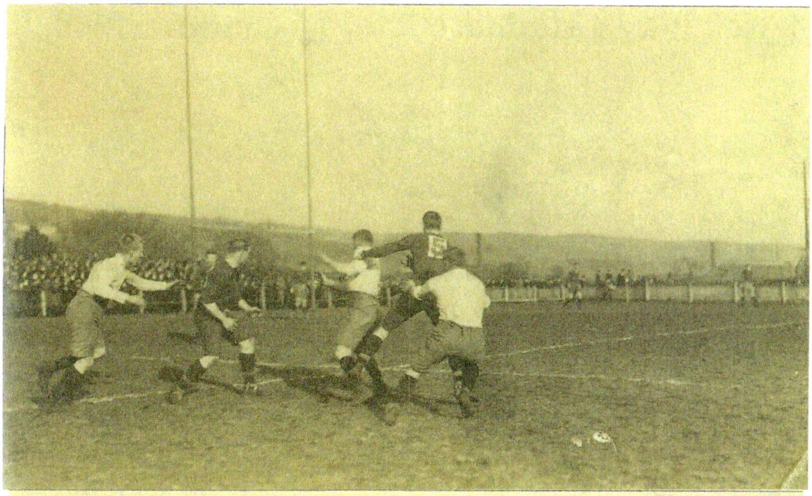

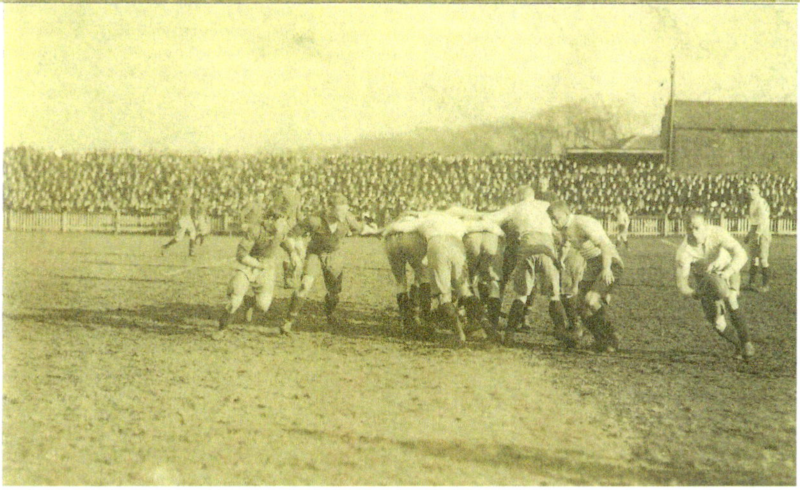

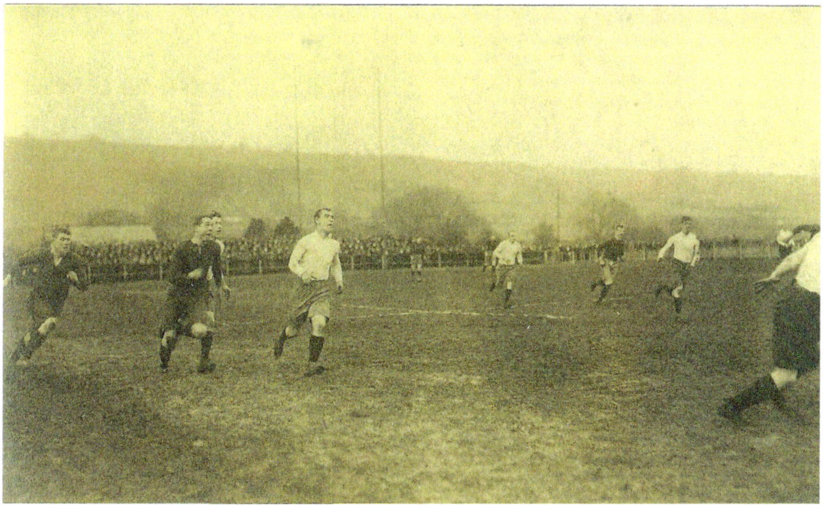

Keighley v Huddersfield, 1st October 1910

Keighley Greyhound Stadium

Originally 'The Beckside Ground' of Parkwood / Keighley Town FC, the greyhounds moved in during 1947, the first meeting being on 22nd November of that year. Keighley Town FC continued to play there until the club folded in 1948, although it was still used as a rugby ground for some years. The stadium closed down at the end of 1974 due to the plans to build the Aire Valley trunk road over the site. The road did come, some 14 years later although a football pitch does now cover the area where the northern part of the stadium lay.

The photograph opposite shows the stadium in its heyday. The old Victoria Park roundabout is located right at the top of the photo.

To the left, one of the very few images (that of a children's sports day) to show that Keighley Town did play at the stadium, the tea hut evident in the background. When the club folded its effects - tea hut *et al* - were sold to a local poultry farmer.

35

The grainy image below shows part of the stadium as it was when it was closed down.

The Greyhound Stadium bus. (From David Busfield flickr). This Albion truck was used to transport the greyhounds from Steeton to the Parkwood track. Busfield says, *'My father took the photo and the man in the photo is his brother Kenneth with my mum. This would have been taken in the late 1940s or early 1950s.'*

King George V Playing Fields, Marley

Formerly the site of allotments, and opened on Saturday 14th July 1956, the famous 'centre pitch' and cinder running track at Marley are both prominent in the two photographs below. Adjacent to the track is the old Keighley RUFC ground. The top photo also shows the Greyhound Stadium in the top right hand corner. There were no 'tip top' pitches at the this time. The bottom photo is dated 1957. Both photos are courtesy of Keighley Local History Society

THE KEIGHLEY NEWS, SATURDAY, JULY 21, 1956

Keighley's new sports centre opened

£19,000 AMENITY WHICH IS FREE FROM DEBT

ONE OF THE FINEST RUNNING TRACKS IN THE COUNTRY

THE fact that Keighley's new King George V Playing Field has included in its layout a well-equipped running track was a special point of mention by those people who participated in the official opening of the Field on Saturday afternoon.

Col. W. W. Shaw-Zambra, a representative of King George's Fields Foundation, who performed the opening ceremony said "This area of land becomes a King George V Field today. The Keighley field is one of some 500 which have similarly been dedicated. In Yorkshire there are 23 fields and the West Riding 18. Although Keighley is one of 500, it is one of a still more select group of King George's Fields—it is one of those which has been provided with a running track. You have got here in Keighley one of the finest running tracks on any of the King George's Fields in the United Kingdom and I do hope you will make the best possible use of it."

A link with the past was the fact that sports had been run on this particular piece of land as long ago as 50 years. But the new track had a link with the future too. He understood that already a young man who that day was taking part in the A.A.A. sports in London had been training on the running track. Perhaps this track at Keighley would play its part in producing Olympic runners of the future.

MESSAGE FROM THE DUKE

Col. Shaw-Zambra read a letter from the chairman of the King George V Playing Fields Foundation and chairman of the National Playing Fields Association, addressed to the Mayor of Keighley. The letter intimated the Foundation's official recognition of the memorial playing field at Keighley as part of the national memorial to his late Majesty, King George V.

There was a message, too, from H.R.H. the Duke of Edinburgh, which was conveyed by Col. Alexander Woods, chairman of the Finance Committee of the National Playing Fields Association. He said the Duke had asked him to convey his congratulations and his good wishes to the people of Keighley on the opening of the playing field.

"As you know," said Col. Woods, "His Royal Highness is very interested in running tracks, and I am very pleased indeed to find this new playing field is equipped with a running track."

Col. Woods said he had brought along with him two very pleasant cheques. One was for £2,500 which came from the

tion, to congratulate all who have been associated with the playing field and with making it possible to be opened without owing a penny to anybody. That is a typically Yorkshire effort and I say that with some pride, because I happen to be a Yorkshireman myself," he said.

The opening of the Butlin Pavilion was performed by Lieut.-Col. A. Basil Brown, a director of Butlins Ltd., who said that not only was he representing the Butlin organisation, but also all the holiday campers and members of the staff who worked together in the scheme through which they tried to assist the National Playing Fields Association. It was essentially a co-operative effort. In the very short time they had

fields was of tremendous importance.

Concluding, he expressed the hope that now they had got a playing field of this quality it would be used. He wanted to see the field played on. "We must participate in the games. We don't want to become a nation of watchers," he said.

Presiding over the ceremony, was the chairman of the Keighley Corporation Parks Committee (Alderman G. H. Norton) who said that as long ago as 50 years a section of the borough had aspiration on this particular piece of land and a programme of sports was held there. In 1921, the first portion of the land was purchased by the town and in 1936 serious steps were taken to provide playing areas for the youth of the town. The town associated itself with the King George's Playing Fields Foundation and a start was made at Highfield. It was then found that for a town of 56,000 this area of

Without him, or a man of his calibre, they would never have got the job done.

As a result he thought they had a running track second to none in England. Everything had been done by the Corporation's own staff. Initially, the programme was to cost £41,000 but eventually £19,000 would be the answer, and today the ground was absolutely free of debt. Keighley was very proud to be in the front in most things and in this latest achievement they had not failed. They were still well to the front among authorities in the provision of playing field facilities for the youth of the town.

Also present were Mr. A. B. Sellers, a representative of the West Riding Playing Fields Association.

The opening was followed by the Secondary Modern School sports meeting. After heavy rain in the morning it was fortunate indeed that the weather remained fine for the whole of the events, although

KEIGHLEY SPORTS GROUND OPENED

Col. W. W. Shaw-Zambra, representing the King George's Playing Fields Foundation, opening the new sports ground at Marley on Saturday. With the speaker is Alderman Norton, chairman of the Parks Committee, and behind, the Mayor and Mayoress of Keighley (Alderman and Mrs. John Taylor), Col. Alexander Woods (chairman of the Finance Committee of the National Playing Fields Association), Lieut.-Col. A. Basil Brown (a director of Butlin's, Ltd.), and Mr. C. R. Hobson, M.P.

The opening of Marley playing fields from *The Keighley News*

Eastburn Cricket Club

The old Eastburn Cricket Club played on a field at the junction of Lyon Road and Green Lane. The club folded when the ground was taken for housing, with Green Close now covering the site. The old pavilion is seen in a later image in this book.

Silsden Cricket Club

Thankfully not one of the defunct sports grounds of Keighley, this old photograph does show the long, gone pavilion and other buildings at Keighley Road.

PAVILION
at
KING GEORGE V
PLAYING FIELDS
KEIGHLEY
WAS MADE and ERECTED
— by —
Ernest Slater Ltd.
Oakworth Road Prepared Joinery Works,
Keighley
(Telephone Keighley 2944)

— Makers of —
PARK SHELTERS and SEATS
ALSO OTHER
PREPARED JOINERY WORK

Kick Off

IN FOOTBALL BOOTS BY ADIDAS, PUMA MITRE, SLAZENGER, ETC.

LITESOME, UMBRO, and BUKTA CLOTHING FROM

WILLIS WALKER
CAVENDISH STREET, KEIGHLEY.

Sutton United FC

This aerial shot of Crosshills has the old Sutton United ground to the bottom right of the image – the goalposts can just be made out. Previously located in the field to the south-west, the club hopped over the wall to the field shown here in 1923. It was shared with Kildwick Parish Cricket Club. However, when the Cricket Club folded in 1930 the footballers had the ground to themselves until United itself folded in the summer of 1956. Within twelve months South Craven School covered the site.

Haworth FC

Haworth's former ground is the 'Old Hall Ground', which was not surprisingly located behind Haworth Old Hall. Efforts to improve the playing area in the 1950s came to little, and by the following decade a revived club was playing at Butt Lane (which can be seen in the top right hand corner of the photo).

The site is still an undeveloped field to the left of Weavers Hill, the Quarry in the photograph now being a public car-park. Haworth Main Street can be seen in the top right hand corner.

TRADING CARDS

J Baines

At the turn of the 1900s, 'Football Cards' were extremely popular. They are also known as 'Trade Cards' as they carried adverts for local businesses on their back. John Baines, who was at different times based in Oak Lane in Manningham, and North Parade and Carlisle Street in Bradford, claimed to be the inventor of these football cards in 1887, six of which could be purchased for a halfpenny.

The first cards portrayed rugby players, but their popularity increased and with the growth of soccer those from that sport were also introduced, alongside those for cricket and golf as well. Baines encouraged the obsession for collecting them among schoolboys by offering prizes to the person who returned the largest number of cards to his North Parade base.

The colourful cards, mostly cut into the shape of a shield, depicted teams, kits, and pen pictures of popular players of the day. Children were also encouraged to write short poems to send to Baines, a selection of which would be printed on the reverse of some shields.

Baines died in 1908 but a son continued the business until 1926, by which time it had located to Barnsley. Many of the cards we find today are in poor condition, with frayed edges. A suggested reason for this is that children would use the cards to play 'Who's nearest?' whereby Baines card would be thrown against a wall and then bounce back onto the pavement.

Baines had his rivals, especially from local firms. WN Sharpe, a local printer and lithographer based on Kirkgate, opposite what was then the City's post office was one such. Sharpe's cards were very similar to the Baines Shields and are now just as collectable. J Briggs, from Leeds, was another rival, and the shaped Keighley Shamrocks one here is one of his.

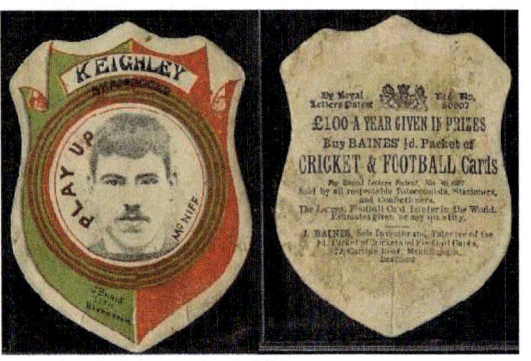

BDV Cigarettes Silks

Around 1900 tobacco companies began to package their products with 'silk' as opposed to cardboard cards in order to lure women to become smokers. Advertisers suggested using these to make useful items for decorating the home. However, they were also cheaper to produce than the normal cards during World War One.

Pinnacle

Pinnacle Cigarettes produced several sets of cards between 1920-23, which included the two rugby players below.

Ogdens

Keighley players featured on the 1926 Famous Players and 1935 Rugby Caricatures sets produced by Ogdens.

Ardath

Cigarette manufacturers Ardath produced several series of sporting photocards in the 1930s. Local teams were invited to send in a photograph, along with team names, and those featured consisted of fully professional clubs alongside minor, short-lived teams. Ardath's 1936 Yorkshire Photocards series included three Keighley teams, all of which are featured below.

Keighley RLFC

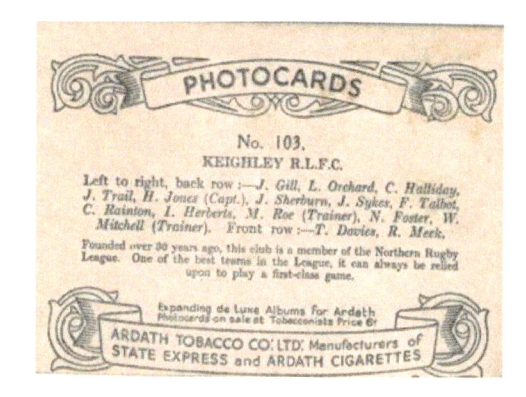

Keighley West Yorkshire FC

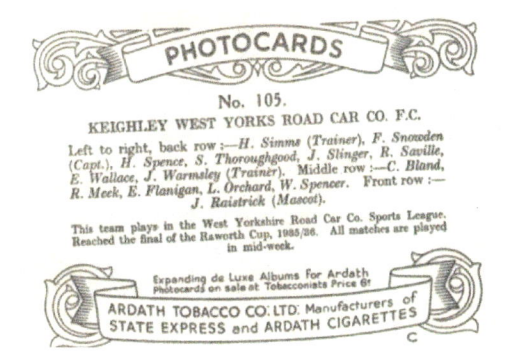

Kildwick Athletic FC

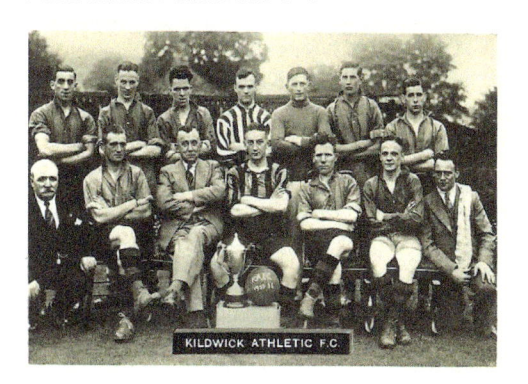

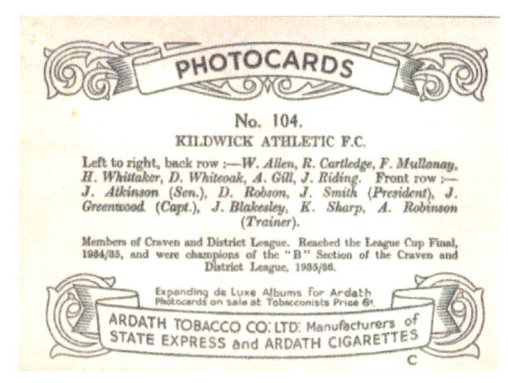

Pin Badges

The number of pin badges that have been assigned to Keighley teams could possibly fill a book in itself. Here are just a few of those produced over the years.

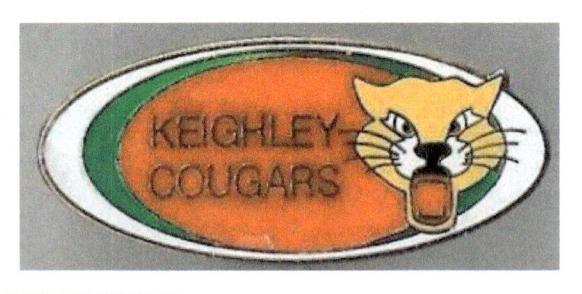

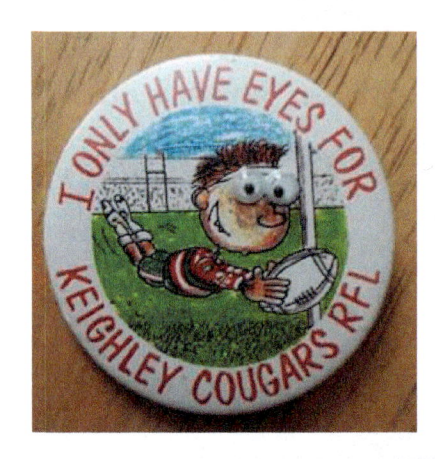

KEIGHLEY SPORTING MEDALS & TROPHIES

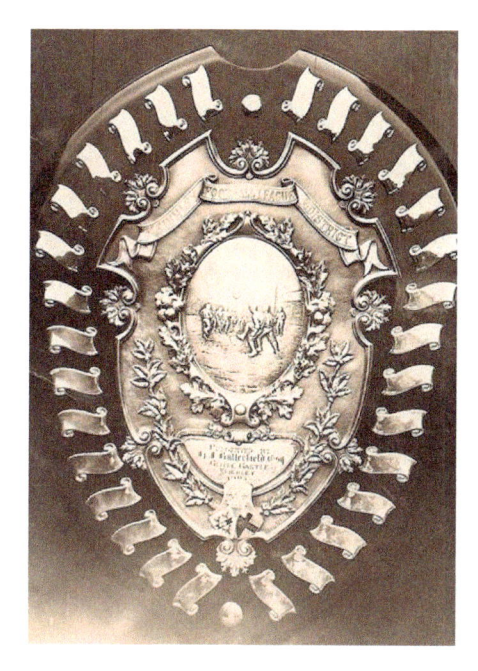

Football

The Butterfield Shield

Henry Isaac Butterfield donated this fine shield to the annual winners of the then newly formed Keighley & District Football League in 1905. It was made by the renowned Fattorini & Sons in Bradford, who produced medals and trophies for teams and competitions all over the world. The shield was a massive piece of silverware, having in its centre a panel with a group of *associationists* (as the *Keighley News* described them) at play. This was surrounded by an oak wreath and a scroll above the centre which bore the name of Mr Butterfield, the Butterfield family crest, and the Keighley coat of arms. This was all mounted on a massive oak frame. Sutton United was the first team to win it.

The Keighley Charity Cup

The Keighley Charity Cup competition was inaugurated in 1886 to raise money for the town's Victoria Hospital. Originally for local rugby teams (the first winners were Silsden) it became a soccer competition in 1904 as interest in rugby waned, Silsden were again the first winners under the new code. The last tournament was in the 1944/45 season but it was revived for two seasons between 1979-81. The trophy had gone missing in the intervening period, but was found in the possession of the Craven Cricket League, who had been presenting to the league's runners-up, minus the footballer statuette on the lid of course. That bit of the trophy was later found in a pile of old dominoes trophies, slightly damaged but well enough to be reunited with the rest of the cup.

Local silverware

The trophies below were won by Arthur Thurling, who played for Guardhouse (and later Keighley Town) in the 1930s, and J Wood, of Worth Village (bottom), who played just after World War Two.

Top left, Keighley Cup 1934/35 winners individual trophy

Top right: Keighley & District League First Division 1936/37 winners individual trophy

Bottom left, Craven League Division One winners 1952/53 individual trophy

Bottom right: Craven FA Cup winners 1952/53 individual trophy

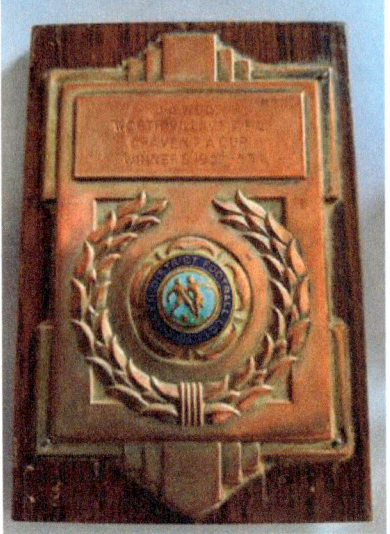

Rugby

Keighley Charity Cup medals are really hard to come by these days.. Above is the one awarded to J Wigglesworth of Ingrow after the 1892 final. His side defeated Keighley Shamrocks by 2 points to nil in the final.

The medal opposite was awarded to R Smith of the Keighley Zingari club after the 1893 final, following a 6 points to nil victory over Ingrow, the holders, in the decider.

The Ingrow team had also appeared in the first Charity Cup final, in 1890, losing to Silsden. It played on at Knowle Spring Brewery upon its formation in 1885 but moved to separate fields on Fell Lane during the intervening years, before folding in 1894.

Cricket

Silsden Craven Cricket Union medal 1897

This is the medal awarded to Silsden's Jack Roberts after his club won the Craven Union Cup that year – the third of six successes between 1891-1901. Silsden didn't actually play in any league competition that season, having withdrawn from the West Bradford League in 1896, and didn't return to league cricket until 1904 when it joined the Craven League (Photos courtesy of Silsden Cricket Club).

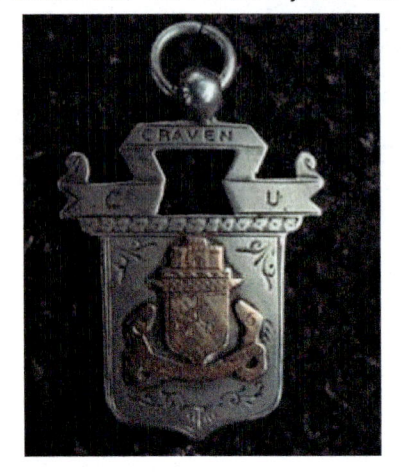

Kildwick Albion 1913 Trophy & Medals

The club finished top of the Skipton & District Cricket League's Second Team Competition that season. Albion was actually the only first team in the league, preferring not to play in the competition's senior division.

Cycling

This is the medal awarded to cyclist Lewis Whitaker (1931-2008) for completing the *'Border and Back'* endurance ride in sixteen hours on 14th August 1954. The medal was awarded by the Keighley Inter-Club Cycling Association (KICA), comprised of the Keighley Road Club, St. Christopher's Cycling Club, Keighley Clarion Cycling Club, Aireworth Cycling Club, Keighley Velo CC as well as Skipton Cycling Club.

Below is another medal awarded to Lewis Whitaker. This one is for completing the Record Ride of 45 1/2 miles in a time of two hours, ten minutes and 45 seconds in 1952. The medal was awarded by the Keighley branch of the Clarion Cycling Club (Both photos on this page courtesy of Margaret and Melissa Whitaker/Keighley Local History Society).

Athletics

In the late 1880s and early 1900s, local sports clubs and associations would organise their own athletics events, held on grass tracks and with good prizes on offer to local winners. The following four cards were won by local runner J B Carr. On their reverse is written the prize that Carr received.

First prize at Queensbury was an 'Electro-plated Spirit Kettle' to the value of £2-15-0. However, Carr exchanged this for a 'Gold Chain & Case for Cigars'. At Glusburn he won a 'Tea & Coffee Service', value £4-4-0. At the Keighley Cycling club events Carr also exchanged the prizes he was expected to receive – in 1902 a 'Walnut 14 Day China Clock', valued at £2-10-0 was swapped for a 'Case of Cutlery'. In 1904 he decided to forgo his cutlery for some 'Pitches Vases'.

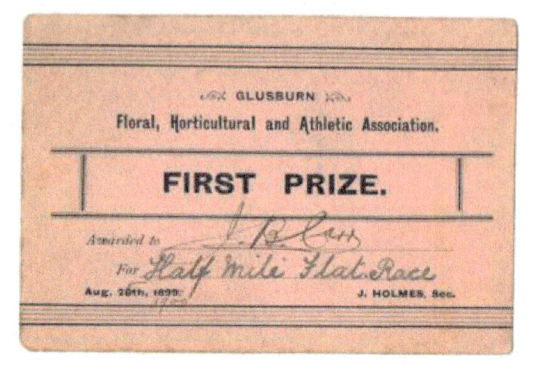

KEIGHLEY & DISTRICT FOOTBALL TEAMS

Wesley Place 1900/01

This early team played at Hainworth, its former ground still used by Ingrow Cricket Club. Among the team's players, John Clough (middle centre) was the son of William Clough, a well-known local mill owner. Billy Thresh is second left at the front & second right at the front is local businessman Bracewell Smith.

Sutton United 1905/06

The team is shown with the Butterfield Shield, awarded to the winners of the newly formed Keighley & District League. United won it at the death after a titanic battle with Keighley Celtic throughout the season.

There was another club from Sutton in the league at the time, the older Sutton Forest FC (who dropped the 'Forest' part of the name right at the start of the season) being the other.

Sutton United Charity Cup Win 1909

The *Keighley Herald* newspaper carried this cartoon following United's 5-1 victory over Cullingworth in the Keighley Charity Cup final, the teams second consecutive victory in this competition.

Isaac Wilkinson Foulds

The Sutton United player is pictured in 1909 with the Keighley Charity Cup and Keighley & District FA Cup trophies.

Sutton United 1907/08 (top) & 1908/09 (bottom)

The team was highly successful in the years before World War One, winning the Keighley League and Charity Cup twice, as well as the first ever Keighley FA cup in 1909. The latter was achieved after a hard fought 2-0 victory over Fell Lane United (photographs courtesy of Malcolm Reid)

Silsden 1904/05

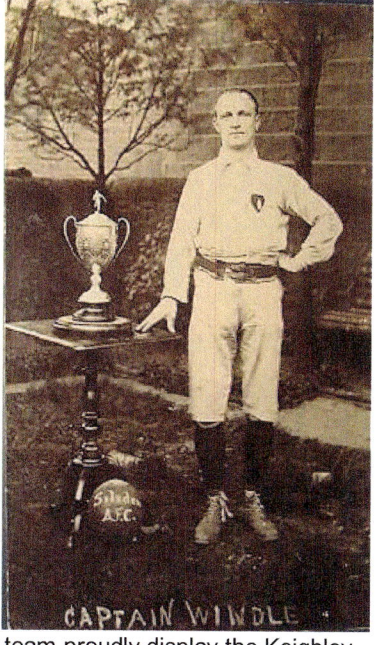

Silsden was also successful in the early years of the sport. Here the team proudly display the Keighley Charity Cup, after winning the inaugural competition with victory over Bingley reserves in the final. Club captain Windle is photographed with the same trophy.

Kildwick 1906

Photographed around 1906, the Kildwick club was a founder member of the Keighley & District League in the 1905/06 season but dropped out after finishing right at the bottom of the league's First Division. It wasn't the end of football in the village though.

Kildwick Old Boys 1910

This photograph is said to have been taken around 1910, when the club was formed as successors to Kildwick FC. It also played in the Keighley League before becoming founder members of the South Craven League in 1922. Renamed Kildwick Athletic in 1924 the club was defunct by 1927.

Cross Roads 1906/07

Two season wonders, the first Cross Roads FC won Keighley League's Division Two South title in the 1906/07 season, spent a season in the top division and then promptly folded.

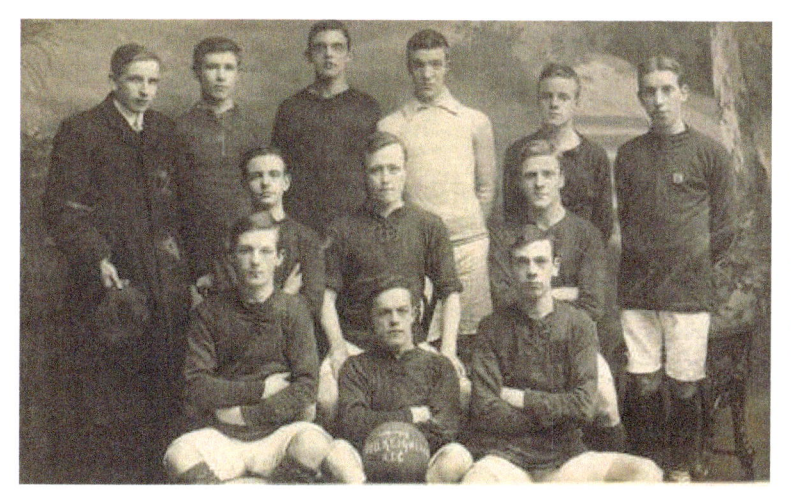

Old Keighlians 1908/09

This team had been around for a year or two before being photographed here. It consisted of local schoolmasters, several of whom helped establish the round ball game in the district.

Keighley Celtic 1908/09

A low quality, but important photograph shows Keighley's first 'super team'. Celtic were Keighley League winners four times, Charity Cup winners five times, and District Cup winners five times in succession in a period between 1905 and the outbreak of World War One. Sadly, the club, which never had a permanent home ground, failed to emerge after the cessation of hostilities.

Victoria Park Brotherhood 1910/11

Undefeated Keighley league Second Division winners in the club's first season, this team, like Cross Roads on the previous page spent just one season in the league's top division before calling it a day.

Ingrow Celtic

This photograph has been dated as 1912/13, although it wasn't until after World War One that a team of that name entered the Keighley League.

Parkwood United Methodist Church 1912/13

This team re-emerged the following year as Parkwood FC. Between the wars the club – following a few name changes – became Keighley Town FC. Dead centre is 'Billy Bott' (William Bottomley) who was sadly one of many local men who were lost in the Great War. Herbert Lake who is possibly seated on the left of the middle row also lost his life around the same time (Courtesy of Andy Wade).

Sutton United 1912/13

By 1913 United was a well established village club, and after the demise of big rivals Sutton FC were the only club in the village. Within 12 months of this photograph being taken they were Keighley League champions for a second time after previous winners Keighley Celtic had moved up to the Bradford & District League.

Silsden 1913/14 (colourised)

The team is photographed with the Keighley Charity Cup, which had been won for the second time (as a football team) following a narrow 3-2 defeat of Cullingworth in the final. Twelve months later they were Keighley League champions before both the league, and the club shut down for the duration of the World War One.

Mytholmes 1920/21

The Mytholmes team was not around for very long, but it is perhaps best known for its remote ground, nicknamed 'The Clarr'. It was located to the flat field adjacent to the river Worth to the left of the bottom of Lord Lane between Oakworth and Haworth. The field, which was also used for cricket, had a pavilion on site for changing, and a goit running through the middle, which had to be covered with turf before each match.

Silsden White Star 1918/19

Keighley Charity Cup winners in the club's first season, White Star defeated Victoria Park 2-0 in the final. The club also competed in the Keighley Junior League among other sides which had to have players with an average age of 18. Two season were then spent in a revived Keighley & District League

Dr John Purcell is in the photograph. He had already started up several sports teams in the town, including Silsden FC.

White Star ran from 1918-21 before being absorbed into Silsden FC, although the name has been revived twice since then.

Back: J T Sutcliffe, H Watson, S Lane, W Downing, G Arkam, R Dover. Middle: J Peel, H Watson, W M Watson (Secretary), W Allen, Dr Purcell, R Spencer, H Driver. Lower: P Shackleton, T Gill, A Bartle, W Fortune, H Hanson (Captain), D Gallagher, H J Walton, A Lund. Sitting: A Inman, W Cooper

Cross Roads 1921/22

This was the re-formed club's first season, and it struggled near the bottom of the Keighley League's Second Division. Two years later the team were Division One champions and twelve months after that was defunct.

Back: W Greenwood, G Gerrard, A Hey, S Pedley, E Slater, F Mitchell, N Hey, A Sunderland (Hon Treasurer), F Bell. Front: A Smales, J Gill, J Hickman, J Longley, J Snaith. Front Two: Herbert Oates, E Feather (Captain) (Courtesy of Adrian Snaith)

Keighley United 1919/20

This team started out as Showfield United during World War One, playing in the Bradford Munitions League. By the 1919/20 season they were runners-up in the revived Keighley League, but the team inexplicably folded during the following season.

Victoria Park 1919-21

Another short-lived Keighley team, Victoria Park played in the Second Division of the Keighley League for just two seasons, finishing runner-up in their section on both occasions. The two photographs here, we can assume, were taken at the end of each of those two seasons.

Keighley St Anne's 1920/21

The photograph above, courtesy of Eddie Kelly, was taken by Bruce Johnson, an esteemed local photographer. It shows St Anne's FC. The bottom photograph is also said to show St Annes, so as this one shows some silverware then this must be at the end of the season after the club had finished top of the Under 21s section of the Keighley League. Sadly the club folded one year later.

Cowling 1921/22

By the time this photograph was taken, Cowling FC had established itself as one of the top five clubs in the Keighley League. The club joined the new South Craven League in the summer of 1922.

Crosshills

Although undated, this is likely to be taken from the 1921/22 season. A Crosshills team took part in the Third Division of the Keighley League that season and finished rock bottom, promptly folding. That team was not related to the current club.

Keighley Charity Cup Final Replay 1921

Local cup finals were well supported. Played at Lawkholme Lane, Haworth v Cullingworth attracted an attendance of 3,500. Cullingworth defeated the Keighley League champions 2-1 in the match.

Caledonian Juniors 1921/22

Caledonians enjoyed a remarkable single season in the Under 16 Division in the Keighley League, winning all but one of its 14 fixtures, to finish well clear of Bingley Rangers at the head of the table.

YMCA Juniors 1921/22

Another Junior team, YMCA had teams in the Senior and Under 16 Divisions in the Keighley League from 1919-24.

Sladen Valley 1921/22

The original Sladen Valley FC emerged in 1919, and was made up of workers constructing the Lower Laithe Reservoir near Stanbury. One year later it was renamed Haworth FC, and promptly won the Keighley League title. However, in 1921 a new Sladen Valley FC was born and by the following season had also taken its place in the Keighley Leagues' top division. However, in the summer of 1923 the club was absorbed into the previous Sladen Valley club, Haworth having recently become founder members of the West Riding County Amateur League (Photograph courtesy of Fred Shuttleworth).

Eastwood 1921/22

There were so many short-lived clubs in the 1920s. Eastwood were winners of the Keighley League's Third Division in the 1921/22 season, only its second year of existence. Promoted to the league's top division for the 1922/23 the club finished a creditable 6th of 12 teams after its double promotion but broke up that summer.

Lawkholme United 1922/23

Formed in 1920, this team folded after having won the Keighley League's Second Division title with an unbeaten record. It is likely that its players were tapped up by the town's better teams in the County Amateur League. It returned for the 1924/25 season but withdrew part way through the campaign.

Morton 1923/24

Morton's successful team won the Keighley League's Second Division title in the 1923/24 season before winning the First Division title in the following two seasons. The team lost only twice in league matches during those three seasons.

Back: H Chapman (treasurer), H Kay, W Slater, W Scaife, C Kay, H Toker, H Hardy, A Bridle, J W Bell (secretary). Middle: B Toker, H Taylor, P Stones, S Oliver, W Briggs. Front: B Wood, H Bell

Keighley & District League Handbook 1923/24

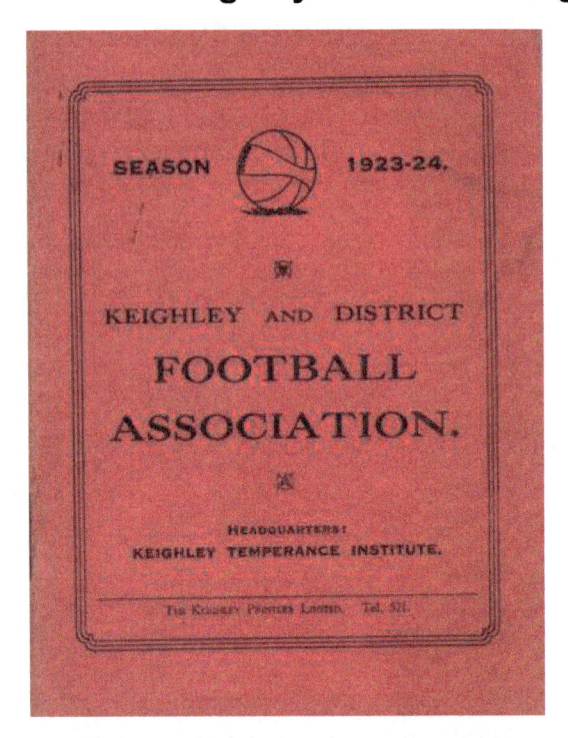

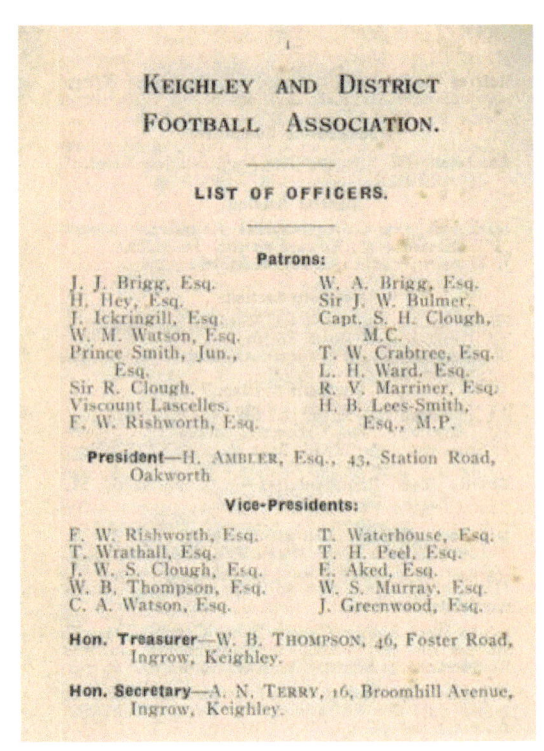

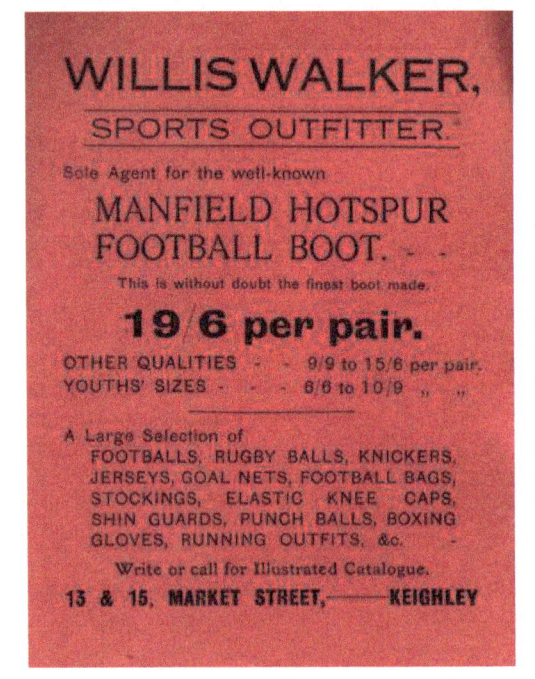

SEASON 1923-24.

KEIGHLEY AND DISTRICT FOOTBALL ASSOCIATION.

HEADQUARTERS: KEIGHLEY TEMPERANCE INSTITUTE.

KEIGHLEY AND DISTRICT FOOTBALL ASSOCIATION.

LIST OF OFFICERS.

Patrons:

J. J. Brigg, Esq.
H. Hey, Esq.
J. Ickringill, Esq.
W. M. Watson, Esq.
Prince Smith, Jun., Esq.
Sir R. Clough.
Viscount Lascelles.
F. W. Rishworth, Esq.
W. A. Brigg, Esq.
Sir J. W. Bulmer.
Capt. S. H. Clough, M.C.
T. W. Crabtree, Esq.
L. H. Ward, Esq.
R. V. Marriner, Esq.
H. B. Lees-Smith, Esq., M.P.

President—H. AMBLER, Esq., 43, Station Road, Oakworth

Vice-Presidents:

F. W. Rishworth, Esq.
T. Wrathall, Esq.
J. W. S. Clough, Esq.
W. B. Thompson, Esq.
C. A. Watson, Esq.
T. Waterhouse, Esq.
T. H. Peel, Esq.
E. Aked, Esq.
W. S. Murray, Esq.
J. Greenwood, Esq.

Hon. Treasurer—W. B. THOMPSON, 46, Foster Road, Ingrow, Keighley.

Hon. Secretary—A. N. TERRY, 16, Broomhill Avenue, Ingrow, Keighley.

WILLIS WALKER,
SPORTS OUTFITTER.

Sole Agent for the well-known

MANFIELD HOTSPUR FOOTBALL BOOT.

This is without doubt the finest boot made.

19/6 per pair.

OTHER QUALITIES - - 9/9 to 15/6 per pair.
YOUTHS' SIZES - - 6/6 to 10/9 ,, ,,

A Large Selection of
FOOTBALLS, RUGBY BALLS, KNICKERS, JERSEYS, GOAL NETS, FOOTBALL BAGS, STOCKINGS, ELASTIC KNEE CAPS, SHIN GUARDS, PUNCH BALLS, BOXING GLOVES, RUNNING OUTFITS, &c.

Write or call for Illustrated Catalogue.

13 & 15, MARKET STREET,——KEIGHLEY

The local league had several local dignitaries in its list of patrons, important businessmen and benefactors such as John Jeremy Brigg (son of former Keighley MP John Brigg, and twin brother of William Anderton Brigg, one time Mayor of the town; Sir Robert Clough, another former MP; James Ickringill, a leading figure in the textile industry and whose brother was also Mayor; Viscount Lascelles, soldier, peer and a son-in-law of King George V.

Parkwood mid 1920s

Since the end of World War One, Parkwood had emerged as one of the district's strongest teams outgrowing the local league. Between 1921 and 1930, there were four District FA Cup victories, three Charity Cup wins, and a Keighley League title in 1922, after which the club played in the West Riding Senior and then County Amateur Leagues. By the 1930s the club had become Keighley Town AFC.

Haworth 1924/25

Founder members of the County Amateur League in 1922, Haworth FC found life difficult in its new surroundings, but persevered in that competition until 1931. Photographed outside its headquarters at The Fleece are: *Back: A Hey, G Gray, B Ferris, A Cole, H Wilkinson, E Hall, J Wilkinson, J Foster, Lister, Jessop, H Walton, H Priestley. Middle: Lister, H Frazer, M Burns, A Earnshaw, Birch, E Lund, T Bowles, L Brown, G Chrichlow. Front: P Wheeler, S Redman*

Haworth Shop 1920s

Although it's only clear if you enlarge this photograph of the old beehive shop on Mill Hey, the plaque to the left hand side of the door is in fact a Haworth FC notice board. It reflects the fact that in this era local sports clubs were supported by the community, which they were very much a part of. Community pride was at its highest when its sporting teams were successful, and local cup finals, for instance, were very well attended by villagers.

Silsden Juniors 1925/26

Photographed in front of the old pavilion at the Keighley Road ground, it's nice to see that generations later the same club is still producing successful junior teams.

Hattersley's United 1929/30

Major employers in the area, Hattersley's was one of the first successful works' teams in the district. Founded in 1924, the footballers played on a ground near Mytholmes and won the Keighley League title in 1930. Its final season was 1939/40, the football club not re-emerging after the war.

Ingrow Crotona 1930/31

Local rivals to the better known Ingrow United, the Crotona club first emerged in 1928 in the South Craven Combination, a competition for teams with an average age of 21. Winners in the 1930/31 season, the club made a big jump up to the Airedale & Craven League, finishing 12th of 14 teams before folding in the summer of 1932.

Wilsden 1930/31

Although, strictly speaking, Wilsden is part of Bradford, its football teams have often preferred to play in Keighley and Craven competitions. The side pictured here did just that between 1930-33, winning the league title at the first attempt after a titanic battle with Ingrow United. The young child in the picture is none other than future England international, Jeff Hall

Keighley Town Minors 1934/35

The club's senior team had just transferred to the Bradford Amateur League, but its Junior team was also successful. The photo is taken at the club's Beckside Ground. *Back: H Hodgson, J Astin, G Bingley, A Little, F Cooke, D Stell, J Critchell. Middle: T Foster, A Thurling, T McDermot (Captain), D Hayton. Front: .Cutter, D Turner, F Thompson*

Oxenhope Recreation 1935/36

It took the village team at Oxenhope, in its various guises, some time to make its mark, but this season saw the club lift the Keighley League's Division Two title ahead of local rivals Denholme United. Twelve months later only Guardhouse prevented Oxenhope from lifting the league's Division One title. The gentleman with the trophy is the future Mayor of Keighley, Joseph Denby.

Guardhouse Sports Club 1936/37

The side won the District Cup, Butterfield Shield & Victory Shield that season. Only the Charity Cup eluded them. Among those pictured are: *T Wildman, J Royston, P Spenser, S Unwin, A Thurling (ex-Keighley Town), W Bell, T McCurry, Peel, E Wilson, B Maddon, E Whittaker, J Marsden, and F Sugden, Mascot: Nilon,*

St. Anne's School 1939/40

Standing: Dennis Timbrell, George Spencer, James Alderson, Jack Bardgett, Terry Nilon, Angela Roddy (Coach). Seated: Frank Wilkinson, Jim Walls, John Kelly, John O'Hara, Jack Farrar (Captain), Noel Sexton, Tom Barrett, Tom McCormack (Courtesy of Eddie Kelly)

St. Joseph's 1941/42

St Joseph's were winners of the Keighley Minor League in the 1941/42 season. *Back: Jimmy Gaffney, Eddie Kelly, Dennis Corbett, Paddy Anderton, Jack Bardgett, Father James Farrell, Joe Storey, Gordon Murray. Seated: Billy McKillican, Bernard Dunne, Kenny Beanland (Captain), John Seed, Jack Hoyle. Front: Geoff Powell, Kenneth Swift.* (Courtesy of Eddie Kelly)

Guernsey School, Lees 1940/41

Refugees from Guernsey arrived in the district during World War Two, with many children being housed at Lees School, Cross Roads. Its football team proved all conquering, winning the Keighley Schools' league and Brigg Cup double, Parkwood defeated 3-0 in the final of the latter competition. Several of its players went on to play for the Keighley Schools' Representative team.

Hattersley's 1941/42

Football did continue some extent during World War Two. A Keighley Interdepartmental League was organised in which a Hattersley's side turned out, against other engineering firms such as Clapham's, Prince Smith's and Dan Mitchell's. Competition must have been fierce if Keighley Town's Tom Hindle (second right, front row) was guesting for them. When he wasn't playing for his Town team he was also playing for Leeds United!

Dean, Smith & Grace 1941/42 & 1942/43

Another team in the wartime Interdepartmental Works League was DS&G. It is interesting to note that the Butterfield Shield was awarded to the league winners.

Sutton United 1946/47

The side is photographed with the Keighley & District Cup (having defeated Silsden 2-0 in the final), and the silverware from the Craven League after winning that title. Twelve months later the team won the Bradford Amateur League title ahead of Haworth (Courtesy of George Walker).

Keighley Town 1945/46

The team is photographed at the conclusion of the final wartime season, in which it took part in the Bradford Amateur league, winning its third league title in six seasons. The following two seasons would see the team competing in the Yorkshire League, alongside the strongest amateur teams in the county and the reserve and third teams of Football League clubs. Misfortune on and off the pitch led to the club's demise in 1948, however. Boxer Percy Vear, the club's fitness coach is third from left on the back row.

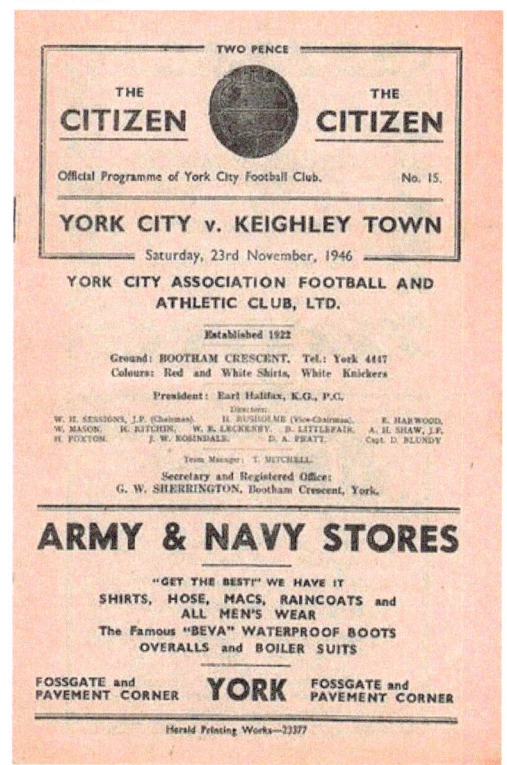

Back: n/k, Jesse Camm, Percy Vear, n/k, Ken Stowell, Walter Farrar, George Hardy, Alf Brown, Jim Farrar, n/k, Edgar Wilson, Vic Dixon. Front: Billy Newman, Billy Hewitt, Jim Thornton, George Walker (Capt), Vic Lewis, n/k, Tom Barrett, George Beaumont

From the Yorkshire League Handbook 1946/47

Keighley Town.
Secretary—Geo. Beaumont, 18 Braithwaite Crescent, Keighley.
Ground—Parkwood Greyhound Stadium, off Dalton Lane, Keighley.
Railway and Nearest Station—Keighley LMS.
Colours—Yellow Shirts, Black Knickers.
Telephone No.—

Leeds United.
Secretary—C. A. Crowther, Elland Road Ground, Leeds 11.
Ground—Bracken Edge, Sycamore Avenue, Harehills Lane, Leeds 8.
Railway and Nearest Station—Leeds, all Coys.
Colours—Blue and Old Gold Halves, White Knickers.
Telephone Nos.—Ground 75112 Leeds. Private 75547 Leeds.

Haworth 1946/47

The team won the first post-war Keighley League title before stepping up to the Bradford Amateur League for a few seasons. *Back: Joe Lister, Ernie Kitson, Cyril Collier, Jim Lowery (Trainer) Benny Grey, Norman Houldsworth, Billy Johnson and G S Phalp. Front: Colin Johnson, Milton Parker, Hartley Greenwell, Jimmy Barnard (capt) Frank Jenkinson, Jack Inman (courtesy of Bob Armstrong).*

Haworth School 1947/48

League champions & Brigg Cup runners-up (Courtesy of Judith Ellis).

You've been picked !

(Courtesy of Eric Robshaw)

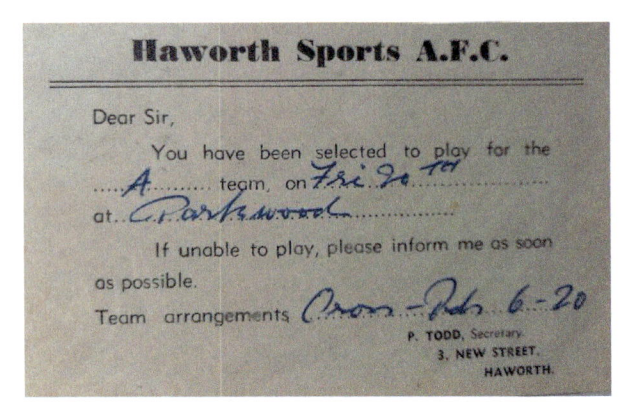

Haworth FC fixture card 1949/50

Bradford Amateur Football League
Premier Division
HAWORTH A.F.C.

Date	Opponent	Venue	Result
Aug. 27	Bradford Electricity	Away	
Sept. 3	Wyke Old Boys	Home	D 2-2
10	Tyersal	Away	L 3
17	U.S.M.P. Co.	Home	L 4
24	Silsden	Away	D 2-2
Oct. 1	St. Joseph's Old Boys	Home	
8	Bingley Town	Away	
15	Wilsden	Home	L 3-4
22	Swain House	Home	
29	Thackley	Away	
Nov. 5	W.R.C.F.A. Cup		
12	Dudley Hill	Home	
19	Local Association Cup		
26	League Cup		
Dec. 3	Frizinghall Rovers	Away	W 9-2
10	Sutton United	Home	
17	Local Association Cup		
24	Larkenshaw		W 6-1
31	Bradford Electricity	Home	
Jan. 7	Wyke Old Boys	Away	
14	Tyersal	Home	
21	U.S.M.P. Co.	Away	
28	Silsden	Home	W 2-1
Feb. 4	St. Joseph's Old Boys	Away	
11	Bingley Town	Home	
18	Wilsden	Away	W 5-3
25	Swain House	Away	
Mar. 4	Thackley	Home	W 5-1
11	Dudley Hill	Away	
18	Frizinghall Rovers	Home	
25	Sutton United	Away	L 0-5
Apl. 1			
8			
15			
22			
29			
May 6			

Bradford Amateur Football League
HAWORTH A.F.C. "B"
Third Division

Date	Opponent	Venue	Result
Aug. 27	Low Moor W.M.C.	Home	W 6-5
Sept. 3	Salts Ltd.	Away	
10	J. T. Hardaker Ltd.	Away	
17	Bradford Gas Dept.	Away	
24	Butterfield's Ltd.	Home	W 4-1
Oct. 1	Bolton United	Away	D 2
8	Bradford City Band C.	Home	L 3-5
15	Local Association Cup		
22	Frizinghall Rovers "B"	Away	W 7-1
29	Tyersal Y.C.	Home	W 3-2
Nov. 5	West Riding Cup		
12	Bulmer and Lumb Ltd.	Away	
19		Home	W 6-0
26	League Cup		
Dec. 3	St. Joseph's Old Boys "B"	Home	W 6-0
10	Ex-Services	Away	W 2-5
17	Local Association Cup		L 0-1
24	Bradford		L
31	Low Moor W.M.C.	Away	L 5
Jan. 7	Salts Ltd.	Home	W 6-1
14	J. T. Hardaker Ltd.	Away	L 1-3
21	Bradford Gas Dept.	Home	
28	Butterfield's Ltd.	Away	W 4-2
Feb.	Bolton United	Home	
11	Bradford City Band "C"	Home	W 5-1
18	Bradford Electricity "B"	Home	L 3-5
25	Frizinghall Rovers "B"	Home	
Mar. 4	Tyersal Y.C.	Away	D 2-2
11	Bulmer and Lumb Ltd.	Home	W 2-1
18	St. Joseph's Old Boys "B"	Away	D 1-1
25	Ex-Services	Home	
Apl. 1	Bradford Electricity "B"	Away	W 3-2
8			
15			
22	Oxenhope v. North Village		9-4
29	Addingham v. Oxenhope		4-1
May 6			

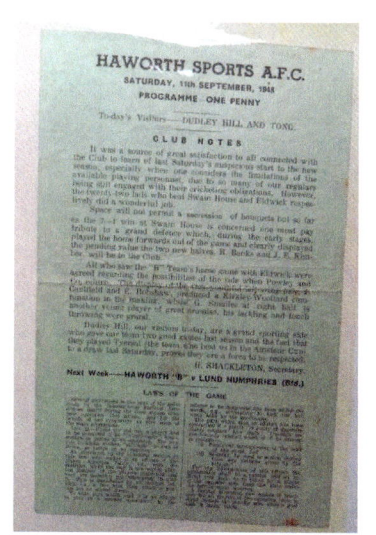

An exceptionally rare Haworth FC programme from September 1948, and ticket for the Keighley Cup final in 1960 (Central won 2-1). All three images of this page courtesy of Eric Robshaw.

Ingrow United

This photograph was taken in the late 40s or early 50s.. United existed from 1930 to 1951, playing in the Keighley and Bradford Amateur Leagues. Their Ingrow Lane ground was in the bottom corner of what is now the Oakbank School site, close to the junction with Bracken bank Avenue. They were Keighley League champions in 1932/33, and 1933/34, and also Keighley Charity Cup winners in 1932/33 when Nelson Amateurs were defeated 3-1 in the final (Courtesy of William Mabbott, whose father Fred is kneeling front right).

Haworth Crowd

This may not be the clearest of images, but what stands out is the size of the crowd in attendance at Haworth around 1950. Village teams were still very much community clubs in those days, and were well supported by the locals (Courtesy of Eric Robshaw)

Newtown Boys Club

Junior footballers at Keighley Gala some time in the 1940s/50s. As far I can gather, the team never did make it to Wembley though. (Courtesy of Keighley & District Local History Society / Celia Allen)

St Anne's 1949/50

Founded in 1946, St Anne's FC won a 17-team single division to become Keighley League champions in 1950, but they withdrew from the competition before the start of the following season.

St Joseph's 1950/51

…whereas St Joseph's FC only played in the 1950/51 season, winning the Keighley League's Victory Shield, defeating league champions Guardhouse 1-0 in the final. Like St Anne's before them, they withdrew from the league just before the start of the following season.

Steeton Minors 1949/50

Photographed with the Keighley Minor League trophy, the team consisted of: *Back: J Fortune, G Hill, D Baxter, E Holmes, D Ivory, C Haffner. Middle: N Briggs, D Yates, D Briggs, B Hudson, M Briggs. Front: G Wright, F Miller* (Courtesy of Steeton AFC).

Oakworth Albion 1951/52

Oakworth's best season saw them achieve a League and Victory Cup double, Oxenhope defeated 3-1 in the final of the latter. It was then this team's turn to fail to reappear the following season, although this was due to the fact that the Keighley League itself went into abeyance for the 1952/53 season. Both club and league returned for the 1953/54 campaign. The league folded for good in 1963, with the nomadic Oakworth club continuing in the Craven League until 1976. Its grounds included fields on Goose Cote Lane, Denby Hill, Ghyll Clough farm, and behind the village Social Club.

Keighley & District League Representative Team 1950/51

Despite the town's top teams having long abandoned the Keighley League, there was still enough strength to put out a representative side against other amateur leagues of a similar standing, such as the Halifax & District League and North Lancashire League. The team is photographed following a 1-4 loss to the latter at Strong Close.

Crosshills Youth Club 1951/52

The club emerged in 1949 with a side in the Craven League, and initially had local rivals Sutton United to contend with until that club faded away in the mid 1950s. By the summer of 1971 Crosshills had dropped the 'Youth Club' suffix, and has of course enjoyed a rich history since then.

Cononley 1951/52

The Cononley club was founded in the early 1900s and had played in various league competitions before becoming founder members of the Craven League in 1934. *Back: Dennis W Robinson, R Blakesley, D Earnshaw, J Armstrong, J Throup, W Duncan. Front: L Blakesey, P Whittaker, G Bell, T Smith, L Mallinson.*

Central Youth Club 1950s

This team first joined the Keighley League in 1953, finishing runners-up behind Worth Village in 1955/56 with the all conquering Keighley Central emerging from the same set-up that summer. *Avove left: Back: Tommy Wilson, John Murray, Ray Geldard, Vinnie Nutter, Michael Boland, n/k. Front: Bobby Heaton, Joe Narey, Brian Coffey, Alan Barton, Peter Lum*

Worth Village 1952/53

The team was newly formed for the 1952/53 season but was immediately successful. It defeated Silsden 4-1 in the District Cup final (with Leeds United's John Charles presenting the cup to the winners) and also won the Craven League title.

(Photograph courtesy of Elaine Tremethick. Programme courtesy of Eric Dawson, who kept goal for Worth Village that day)

Worth Village 1955/56

This was the club's final season. After winning the Keighley League title the teams' players dispersed to other local clubs.

Back: Albert Naylor, Stan Storton, Denis Cooney, Tommy Green, Alan Brunskill, Billy Rooke. Front: Barry Davidson, Peter Cawthorne, Bernard Fletcher, Colin Longley, Tommy Anderson, Joey Green.

Silsden v Bradford City 1951 Friendly

Silsden 1951/52

Silsden won the District Cup, and finished runners-up in the Wharfedale League this season. The club's second team won a league and cup double in the same league, which was the club's first in this competition.

Silsden 1955/56

Silsden's reserves playing in the snow v Gargrave. Would this match have been played in these conditions modern times?

Keighley Shamrocks 1960/61

The Shamrocks name burst back onto the scene when the team won the Keighley League at the first time of asking in the 1956/57 season. The title was defended the following year, with the team moving into the Bradford Amateur League in 1958. Shamrocks were promoted to that league's First Division at the end of the 1960/61 season, its team photographed here.

Back: Bob Livesey, Joe Lowe, Michael Boland, Mick McCartney, Vinnie Nutter, Leo Pullich, Colin Butler. Front: Peter Wood, Frank Bland, Tony Bland, Alan Thornton, Norman Barton.

Steeton 1961

At the time, Steeton FC was a well-established Craven League team. *Back: W Hodgson, D Baxter, D Minney, R Cox, A Bates, J Newton, J Fortune. Front: M Hainsworth, M Mosley, T Briggs, T Williams, P Reape, B Hill.*

Keighley Lifts 1961/62

The Lifts team at the time featured a young Maurice Tillotson who went on to enjoy a successful career in New Zealand (Courtesy of Eric Malcolm Binns).

Back: Hogg, Malcolm Pullen, Trevor Powell, Bryan Wilson, Lynford Tretton, Maurice Tillotson. Front: Barry Hill, John Bibby, Ron Pritchard, Stuart Banks, Stuart Harrison

Keighley Lifts 1962/63

The summer of 1962 saw Lifts move from the ailing Keighley League into the Craven League (Courtesy of Eric Malcolm Binns).

Keighley Lifts 1963/64

Photographed with *Miss Keighley Lifts*, this team includes, back, right, former professional footballer Harr Haddington, and Farrell Butler (front, second from right) who was one of Keighley's finest Comedians & after dinner speakers. His book *The Comedy of Heroes* recounts his tales of meeting sporting celebrities (Courtesy of Eric Malcolm Binns).

Guardhouse 1964

The re-formed Guardhouse club competed in the Bradford Red Triangle League, as well as the Keighley Junior League for the 1963/64 season.

Haworth Youth Club 1959/60

The team went on to play in senior football in 1963, eventually dropping the 'Youth Club' suffix to become the latest to play as Haworth FC. This photo is from the Vine Tavern Collection. *Back: Frank Haigh, Tag Bottomley, D Squires, Mick Williamson, David Bairstow, Harry Haigh (manager). Front: n/k, Ken Richardson, Geoff Berry, John Bibby, Stewart Harrison, John Sunderland.*

Oxenhope Recreation 1966

Oxenhope was the leading team in the Craven League in the early and mid-1960s, with a host of league and league cup victories

Keighley Central, League Cup Final 1963/64

The 1960s were all about Keighley Celtic. The 1963/64 season was spent in the Yorkshire League, where the club played in the Third Division. The title was won, but there was defeat to Farsley Celtic reserves in the League Cup Final, which was played at Salts.

Sadly that was the only season in which Central played in the Yorkshire League as the Third Division was dispensed with in the summer of 1964 and facilities at Marley prevented the club from being promoted to a higher division.

Keighley Central 1966/67

The club's first and second teams, who both played in the West Yorkshire League are featured here. *Back: D Sturdy, C House, M Beck, S Magee, R Cox, D Wellock, F Bland, D Palamountain, R Lister, R Butterfield, B Spencer, R O'Hanlon, R Hobson, J Bland. Front: P Boland, T Wilson, N Creighton, G Riley, T O'Hara, D McGowan, W Butterfield, A Hockey, J.Bibby, J Parker, J Clark,*

How many people have a copy of Trevor Hockey's 7" single, released in 1968?

Keighley Central Programme 1964/65

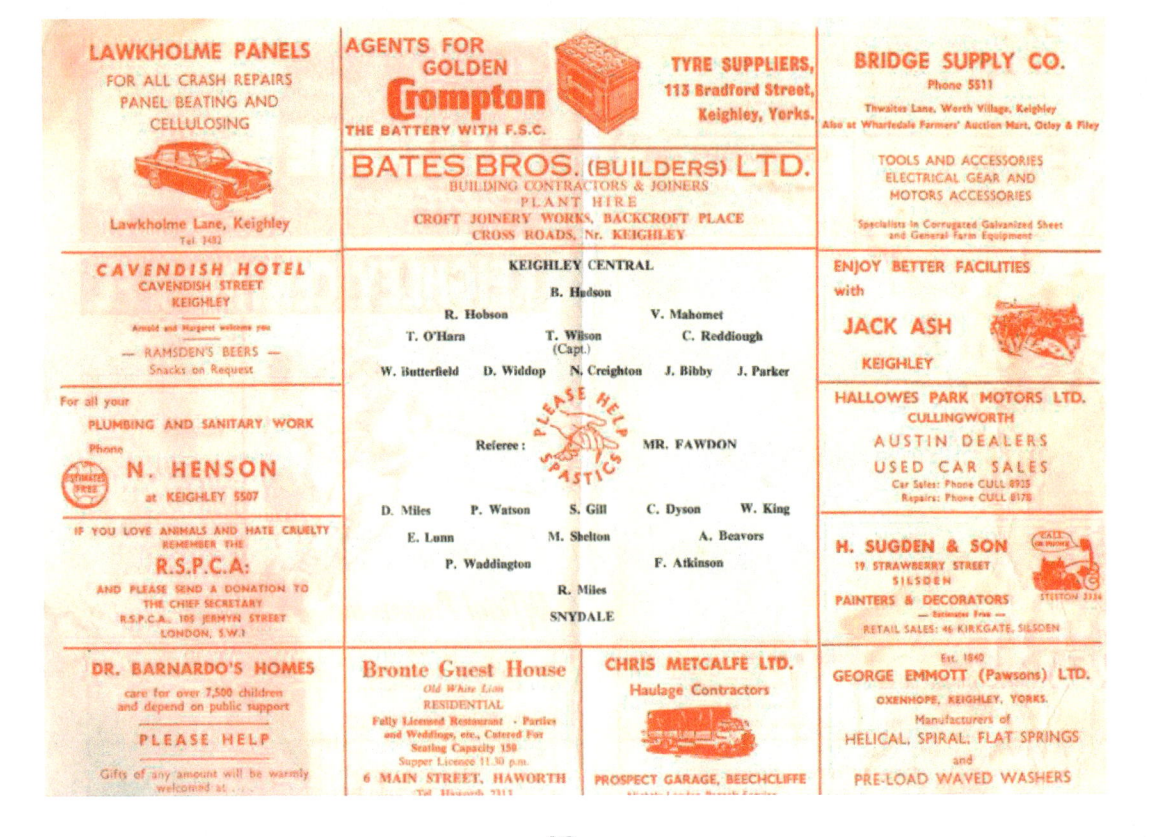

KEIGHLEY CENTRAL

B. Hudson
R. Hobson — V. Mahomet
T. O'Hara — T. Wilson (Capt.) — C. Reddiough
W. Butterfield — D. Widdop — N. Creighton — J. Bibby — J. Parker

Referee: MR. FAWDON

D. Miles — P. Watson — S. Gill — C. Dyson — W. King
E. Lunn — M. Shelton — A. Beavors
P. Waddington — F. Atkinson
R. Miles

SNYDALE

Keighley Central 1967/68 County Cup winners

Central became the first Keighley team to win the West Riding County Cup. Brook Sports were defeated 2-1 in a replayed final at Thackley following a 1-1 draw. John Fay scored the first Central goal on the night, before being stretchered off with a broken leg, with Danny McGowan scoring the winner against their Heckmondwike-based opponents.

Keighley Central 1972/73

This is possibly the last photograph taken of the team before it folded at the end of the season.

Back: R Dugdale. J Hellawell, J Caulfield, C Murray, B McGuinness, R Lister, J Parker. Front: M Hockey, C Storton, A Hockey, D McGowan, P Anderson.

Keighley NSF Rangers 1965/66

Playing in the County Amateur League, the team is photographed after their final, and most successful season in that competition. *Among those in the photograph are coaches Roy Brook (front left) and Tommy Hindle (centre, second left), and players such as John Fay, Richard Dugdale, Vic Mahomet, Jack & David Hobson, Eddie Whitaker, Jimmy Walsh, Dennis Baxter & Pat Boland*

Dean Smith & Grace 1966/67

Sunday football arrived in Keighley in 1961, with the formation of the Keighley Sunday Alliance. DSG came along three years later and completely dominated the league until the club folded in 1971. Regular entry was made into the English Sunday Cup, with a run through to the semi-final in the 1966/67 season. The team that defeated Birmingham-based Bromford in a replayed quarter final is featured here. Note the size of the crowd at Marley in the second photograph.

Keighley Shamrocks 1967/68

Shamrocks are photographed here following the club's league and cup double in the West Yorkshire League.

Coaches Roy Brook & Tommy Hindle had achieved success with NSF two years earlier, as had several of the players, many of whom later achieved yet more success at Silsden.

Back: T Powell, R Dugdale, T Hindle, T Fudge, B Hanson, Jack Hobson (captain), V Nutter, D Thwaites, David Hobson, S Brook. Front: Bob Hobson, T Boland, L Pullich, K Heaton, R Peacock, R Brook.

Prince Smith & Stells 1966/67

Prince Smith's ran teams in several sports, with its own sports ground on Dalton Lane. The footballers are photographed following their promotion to the Premier Division of the Craven League.

Keighley Post Office 1968/69

GPO played in the Keighley Sunday Alliance from 1965-69. *Back: Don Kirkley, Brian Maiden, Colin Duckworth, Ben Laycock, Vic Mahomet, Tony Jolly. Front: Derek Kirkley, Roland Wood, Colin Ward, Patrick Foy, Walt Jessup* (Courtesy of David Kirkley)

Crosshills 1970/71

Thanks to the scoring exploits of Jim Fenton, the side, coached by John Hellawell, won the Craven League title, and remained undefeated throughout its league campaign. John himself, brother of Mike, had played in the Football League for Bradford City, Rotherham United & Darlington.

Silsden 1971/72

Taken prior to the side's 4-0 victory over Cowling in the Keighley Cup Final, the team had already secured the West Riding County Amateur League title.

Heaton's around 1970

Heaton's were members of the Keighley Sunday Alliance between 1967-71. This photo is from the Vine Tavern collection.

Back: Dave Howker, Mark Ginley, Pete Ratcliffe, Carl Storton, Brian Cowling, Barry Turnbull, Rennie Butterfield. Front: Terry Cusker, Phil Butterfield, Colin Isherwood, Alan Cowling, Pete Dawson.

Early Magnet

Dean Smith & Grace became the first Keighley team to win the County Sunday Cup in the 1970/71 season. At that time Magnet FC was playing matches in the Second Division of the Keighley Alliance…

Magnet 1971/72

…and then when DS&G folded, its players decamped to Magnet, where they continued to win lots and lots of silverware. Here they can be seen celebrating their 4-0 victory over Holycroft in the league's Kensington Cup final. This was on top of Magnet's inevitable promotion to the league's top division. Twelve months later they were Keighley Sunday Alliance champions.

Prince Smith & Stells 1971/72

The team was promoted to the Craven League's Premier Division after having run away with the Division One title, winning 20 of its 22 fixtures, drawing the other two.

Back: Stuart 'Bert' Woolley, R Pennington, T Cusker, G Sutcliffe, R Maghee, H Wellock, S Natinzic, N/K. Front: A Cowling, F Farrington, P Butterfield, J Woodburn, Mostyn Hockey.

Silsden United 1973/74

The team won the Third Division of the Keighley Sunday Alliance, on goal average from Tong United

Silsden United 1977/78

United moved to the Wharfedale Sunday League in 1975. The club effectively became Silsden FC's Sunday team in 1978.

Keighley Town '79

Trevor Hockey returned home and reformed Keighley Town FC in 1979. The team was accepted into the West Riding County Amateur League for the 1980/81 season. The team is shown here prior to its local derby at Highfield against Keighley Shamrocks. *Back: Derek Nixon, N/K, Jack Hobson, Alan McGuiness, Bob Lee, David Hobson, Jeff Cummins. Front: Barney Maude, Ian Greenwood, Keith Lowe, Alan Hockey, Jimmy Bland, Trevor Hockey, Peter Turbitt.*

Silsden 1981/82

A new look Silsden FC was back in the Craven League by the early 1980s. The 1981/82 season saw the team pipped to the league title by Barrowford United, with Steeton just two points in arrears.

Keighley Town '79 1982/83

West Riding County Amateur League Premier Divisions champions at the first attempt. The team had spent the previous two seasons at the top of Division One, denied promotion the first time around due to ground grading issues. The club's reserve team won the league's Division Two title the same season.

Back: Bob Taylor, John Mitchell, Jeff Cummings, Andy Isherwood, Dave Robinson, Eddie Newton, Jimmy Bland, Alan Hockey, Derrick Nixon. Front: Andy Burrows, Andy Gaughan, Peter Turbitt, Keith Lowe, Kevin Bailey and John Dembijiky.

Greenhead Youth Club 1981

Greenhead's five-a-side team that took part in the NAYC North Eastern Regional Championship at Cleckheaton. *Back: Philip Wood, Dale Parnham. Mike Breeze, John Nixon. Front: Darren Whitaker, Paul Smith, Dale Scott* (Courtesy of Mike Breeze).

Utley 6-a-side competition.

Taken around 1982, this photo contains some of Keighley's best known local soccer players at the time, The team name is lost in the mist's of time, their shirts borrowed from the Green Gables Sunday league team. *Back: Darren Whitaker, Richard Dugdale, Paul Hollindrake. Front: Tom Hey, John Fay, n/k.* (Courtesy of Darren Whitaker)

Greenhead Grammar School Under 16 Girls

The school's five-a-side team won the Bradford metro title early in 1983. From left to right: *Joanne Horton, Julie Blades, Tracy Kirk, Rhona Robinson, Susan Brewer and Rachel Pressley.*

Lothersdale Athletic 1981/82

Formed in 1935, Lothersdale FC originally played on a field in the village made up of two former fields, known as *The Holme* and *Holmleigh Meadows*. By the 1981/82 season the team was struggling in the lower reaches of the Craven League. Ironically the team folded following one of its most successful years, when it won the Craven League's Division One title in the 2002/03 season but was unable to take its place in the Premier Division the following season. It had become harder to attract players to the club, which had decamped to Marley from its former ground several years earlier.

Juventus 1982/83

The 1982/83 season saw Juventus finish as runner-up in the Keighley Sunday Alliance's Second Division. Founded as AC Alassio in 1976, the team changed its name to Juventus the following season, before spending its final season playing as Villa Roma in 1986/87.

Keighley Minors 1981/82

Photographed on the old Marley centre pitch. *Back: Paul Symonds, Phil Wood, Ray Bradley, Sean McNulty, Neil Harrison, Greg Tillotson, Steve Lampkin, Steve Hall. Front: Darren Whitaker, Shaun Bonner, Tony French, Dale Scott, Dave Newbould, Steve Reynard and Paul Smith.*

Brontë Ladies' 1982

This photo shows the club founder and manager Bill Roper and team captain Maureen Kerry following the team's success in a tournament in Spain in February 1982. Inaugurated in 1968, Brontë became one of the country's leading women's teams in the 1970s and '80s and was a founder member of the National Women's League in 1991, at which point the team moved from its ground at Marley to Salts FC.

Cyprane 1982/83

Founded in 1980, the team proved successful with successive Craven League Second and First Division titles in the 1981/82 and 1982/83 seasons. A year was spent in the Premier Division before the club folded in the summer of 1984 having initially been accepted into membership of the County Amateur League.

Keighley Lifts 1982/83

The team had entered the Craven League in 1970, playing in the competition until it folded in 1983, by which time it was more than holding its own in the Premier Division. The club did return six years later (Courtesy of Neil & Paula Barnes).

Silsden 1983/84

The club's Sunday team had established itself as a leading team in the Wharfedale Sunday League by now. Having won the Keighley Sunday Cup the previous season, the team were defeated by Bradley's in the 1983/84 final.

Back: Colin Guest, Richard Cleaver, Kevin Barret, Kevin Knappy, Alan Larkin, Ian Guest. Front: Sam Whitaker, Andy Geary, Bob Craven, Kevin Rooke, Mark Houfe.

Haworth 1984/85

Haworth FC had endured a few years of struggle before being promoted back to the Premier Division of the Craven League in the summer of 1984. The 1984/85 season saw the side become close to winning the league title, finishing just a point behind Barnoldswick United and Gargrave. Twelve months later the team finished runner-up to Colne United before rejoining the County Amateur League. The team is photographed at its old Butt Lane ground behind the school.

Oxenhope Recreation 1984

Back: Ian Dyson, Rick Barton, Des, Paul Barnes, Neil Barrett, Paul Brearey. Front: Ashley 'Beefy' Bevan, Jonnie Coates, Andy Burrows, Bill, Phil Hoggard, Ian Jowett.
(Courtesy of Neil Barrett)

Oxenhope Recreation 1985/86

By the mid 1980s, Oxenhope's glory years were temporarily behind them, but the team maintained its position in the top division of the Craven League.

ST Autoparts 1986/87

Seen celebrating its Keighley Sunday Alliance Third Division title at the end of the club's final season, ST Autoparts bowed out in style. Founded as Pak Kashmir in 1980, the team played as Devonshire Park FC between 1981-84, before adopting the name of its sponsor in its final three seasons.

Silsden 1986/87

Keighley Town's local dominance had ended, and it was Silsden's turn to be top dogs. For the time being at least. The team finished in seventh place in the Premier Division of the County Amateur League this season, with Keighley Town finishing rock bottom.

Silsden Town 1986/87

In the Sunday game, Wharfedale Triangle side Silsden Town became top dogs, 1986/97 seeing the first of three successive Keighley Sunday Cup final victories. Magnet were defeated in the 1987 final, with Black Horse defeated in the final in the following two seasons.

Highfield 1986/87

The 1986/87 season was Highfield's first in the Wharfedale Sunday League, following four league titles in five seasons (the first two as Timothy Taylor's FC) in the Keighley Sunday Alliance.

Black Horse 1989/90

The team began as Volunteers Arms in the Keighley Alliance, becoming Royal FC and then Black Horse in 1986. It remained unbeaten in the Wharfedale Sunday League in the 1987/88 season yet lost the title on goal difference to Bolton Woods. The team became Keighley Star in 1990, achieving massive success in local competitions until folding in 1996.

Cononley Sports 1988/89

Relegated from the top division of the Craven League in 1987, Cononley held their own in the second tier before being promoted back to the Premier Division in 1992.

Haworth 1989/90

Haworth players are pictured following the team's 1-0 victory in the Keighley Cup final. Goalscorer Richard Clarkson is in the middle of the back row. It was only the second, and last, time the club won the District Cup.

Airedale Magnet 1990/91

Magnet defeated Druids Arms 2-1 in the 1990/01 Keighley Sunday Cup final, and finished the 1990/91 season as runner-up in the Wharfedale Sunday League for the second season in succession, this time behind Star Athletic. Switching to the Wharfedale Triangle the following season, Magnet turned the tables on Star to lift the title, the club's last before it folded in 1993.

Keighley FA Officials 1990

Featured with the West Riding County Minor Cup are *Mike Breeze, Bill Hook, John Nevison, Jack Holmes, Tony Atherton, Bryan Pamment, Andy Brook, Dennis Coburn, and Peter Pamment.* Keighley defeated Heavy Woollen FA 3-1 in the final thanks to a hat-trick from Owen Malcolm.

Boltmakers 1991/92

At one time sponsored by Oasis, due to team member Roger Nowell's involvement with the band, the team is seen in its first season in the Keighley Sunday Alliance. The team switched to the Wharfedale Sunday League in 1996 and was renamed AC Victoria in 2003, achieving massive local success under that title before folding during the 2009/10 season.

Keighley FA Minors 1993/94

Keighley's representative team became County Champions for only the third time in 1994. Craven FA were defeated 2-0 in the final of the County Minor Cup, which was played at Steeton, thanks to double from Daniel Gaudiosi. The Keighley FA squad for the final was *M Foulger, A Reed, D Gaudiosi, D Wilkinson, M Watson, R Holmes, A Suttlewood, N Wojtas, R Pearson, J Smith, M Morrell, D Watson, G Florence, J Anderson, and G McLafferty.*

Haworth 1990/91

Haworth FC was running three senior teams during the 1990/91 season, but the club's enforced move away from the village to play home games at Marley proved disastrous and the club folded altogether during the 1999/2000 season.

Grafton Garage 1986

Founded in 1984 Grafton won the Craven League's second tier at a canter at its first attempt. After a fifth place Premier Division finish in 1985/86 the team became the first to be expelled from the league for persistently poor discipline. The team continued for a short while in the Bradford Red Triangle instead.

Crossroads Inn 1988-92

Crossroads had made it way up to the Craven League's Premier Division - with a Division Two title along the way – before folding after finishing in mid table in the 1991/92 season.

Druids 1994/95

One of Keighley's most successful teams in the late 80s and 1990's, Druids (formerly Beeches) celebrate winning the Wharfedale Sunday League title. The team became Keighley Athletic in 1998.

Crosshills 1995/96

Crosshills lifted the District Cup for the second year in succession, with a narrow 2-1 victory over Haworth. The team was by now playing in the top of the East Lancashire League.

Keighley Shamrocks

Shamrocks' Sunday league team was formed in 1984, and continued when the Saturday team folded. Pictured here in the early 1990s, the team won the Keighley Alliance title in the 1990/91 season, before moving to the Wharfedale Sunday league. After three seasons in that competition the team sadly folded.

St Anne's Celtic 1995/96

Founded in 1989, the St Anne's team is seen celebrating its third consecutive title in the Keighley Sunday Alliance. The team moved to the Wharfedale Sunday League after, winning that title twice before returning to the Keighley competition for one last season in 2000/01. The team is best known for making its way to the County Sunday Cup final in the 1996/97 season, losing to Bolton Woods, and winning the Keighley Sunday Cup for the first and only time the same year.

Steeton 2001/02   West Riding Challenge Trophy Winners

Steeton lifted the County Trophy under the guidance of Jez Fay after coming from two-goals down to defeat Hunsworth 3-2. James Gill, Daniel Gaudiosi and a late, late strike by Steven Barker were enough to see the Summerhill Lane side to victory. Since then Roy Mason has led the club to the dizzy heights of the North West Counties League.

Keighley Phoenix

For a few years in the late 1990s and early 2000s, Keighley Phoenix was one of the strongest teams in the West Riding, with a County Amateur League title and some near misses in the County Cup. Emerging from the Greenhead Youth Club team in the 1980s, Phoenix initially played in Sunday football before entering the County Amateur League in 1991. By 1998 the team was in the Premier Division, with the league title won in the 1999/2000 season, just a single point ahead of Hemsworth MW and Campion. Silsden were defeated 1-0 in the Keighley Cup final that season too, Phoenix's third successive win, and fourth in total, in that competition. The team was at the pinnacle of its success, and as Silsden re-emerged from the shadows, Phoenix's time at the top was relatively short-lived.

Keighley Juniors 2001/02

Sunday teams in Keighley were also successful, with Juniors, founded in 1991, winning the Wharfedale League and Cookson Cup double before moving on to the Bradford Sunday Alliance.

Silsden

Silsden's Saturday team was revived in 1996. By 2004 it had secured election to the North West Counties League following an incredible rise through the ranks of the Craven League and the West Riding County Amateur League, winning the West Riding County Cup three seasons in succession along the way.

2000/01

The team won the County Amateur Division One title to gain promotion to the Premier Division. Phoenix were also toppled in the Keighley Cup final.

County Cup winners 2002

Jimmy Hedges scored the winner against Campion at Woodlesford, marking the first of three successive wins in the competition. (Courtesy of David Brett)

Martin Bland's promotion winning 2005 goal

In the second half of the final game of the 2004/05 season, Bland rose to head home the winner against Cammell Laird at Cougar Park to see Silsden promoted in their first season in the North West Counties League (Courtesy of David Brett).

Teams would go to great measures to try to stop Silsden from winning (Courtesy of David Brett)

Brontë Wanderers 2006/07

Brontë won the Keighley & District Cup for the first and only time with a 2-1 win against Keighley Shamrocks. The team also won the Division Two title in the County Amateur League that season.

AC Victoria 2007/08

Jeff Hall Cup Winners in 2008 following a 2-1 victory over new Varity Club, AC Victoria also won the Keighley Sunday Alliance title for a third successive year and reached the Keighley Sunday Cup final, losing 1-3 to Silsden.

Stanbury Park Rangers 2000/01

One year after having won the Keighley Sunday Alliance with a 100% record, Stanbury won the Wharfedale Sunday League title with another unbeaten record, ahead of both Keighley Juniors and Silsden.

Players: *S Turkington, D Labbett, N Rollins, D Bainbridge, G Ellis, S Waddington, C Labbett, M Labbett, C Horsefield, M Thompson Smith, S Thompson (captain), S Bainbridge, M Sugden* (Courtesy of Steve Bainbridge).

Stanbury Park Rangers 2008/09

The team is photographed here in its final season, after having finished in third place in the Keighley *Sunday Alliance.*

Players: *A Ryan, R Andrew, N Rollins, D Bainbridge, D Ward (Captain), D Head, J Gilmartin, T Pawson, S Bainbridge, D Armstrong, S Perryman, L Best, B White, M Nazir, M Gilmartin* (Courtesy of Steve Bainbridge).

Keighley Ladies 2010/11

West Riding Women's Division One Champions in the 2010/11 season, the team won the Premier Division title the following season. Rebecca Kenna, sat to the left of the goalkeeper of course now excels at Snooker (Courtesy of Gail Hanson).

Cowling 2010/11

This was a successful era for Cowling, who lifted the Keighley Cup in 2009/10, twelve months after having won the Craven League's Division One title. The team then finished runner-up in the Craven League's Premier Division for three successive seasons between 2009-12.

Oxenhope Recreation 2011/12

Oxenhope made the jump up to the West Yorkshire league in 2008, and by the summer of 2011 had been promoted to the Premier Division as Division One champions. Here they are seen after having defeated Cross Hills 7-4 in an amazing Keighley Cup final at Silsden. It was the club's first victory in the competition since 1966.

Things would get even better for Oxenhope, who lifted the West Riding County Cup in 2015.

Brontë Wanderers 2011/12

The team was in the First Division of the West Riding County Amateur League this season, which proved to be the club's last. Attempts to upgrade the vacant Butt Lane pitch in Haworth to league standards had earlier proved unsuccessful.

Sporting Keighley 2021/22

In more recent years Sporting Keighley FC rose up the Craven League, establishing itself in the league's Premier Division, before making an unsuccessful step up to the West Yorkshire League. (Courtesy of the club's Twitter/X page)

Alan Feather & Jack Holmes

Alan and Jack were two of Keighley's longest serving and well respected officials for several decades in the 1990s and into the 2000s (Courtesy of David Brett).

A selection of Keighley & District club match day programmes from more recent times

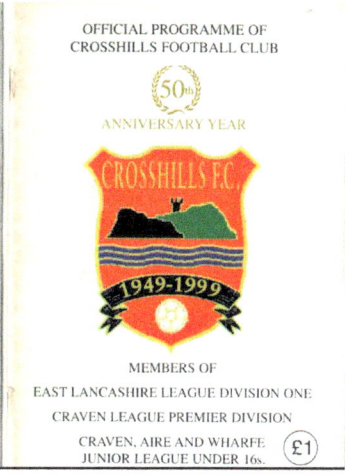

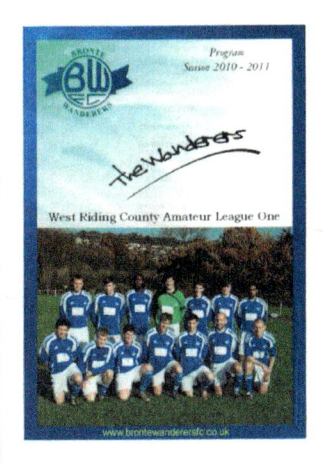

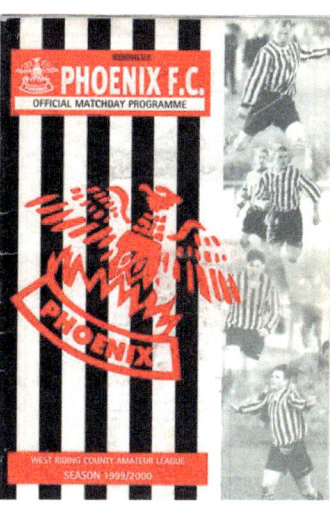

Crosshills, Oxenhope, Brontë Wanderers, and Keighley Phoenix have all been regular issuers in the past. Brontë and Phoenix are sadly now no more.

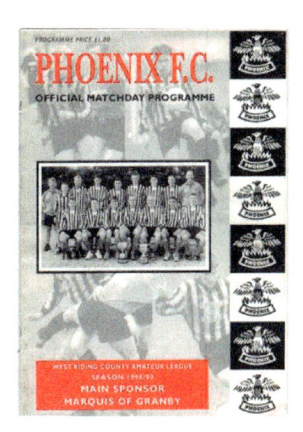

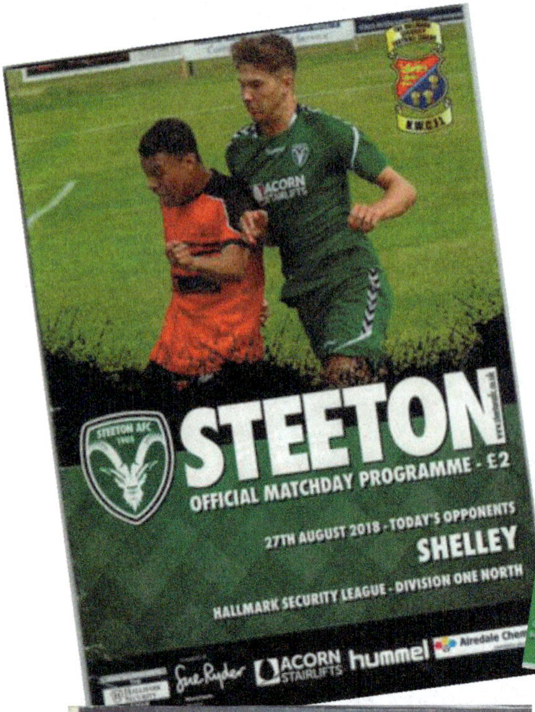
STEETON
OFFICIAL MATCHDAY PROGRAMME - £2
27TH AUGUST 2018 - TODAY'S OPPONENTS
SHELLEY
HALLMARK SECURITY LEAGUE - DIVISION ONE NORTH
ACORN STAIRLIFTS
hummel

STEETON AFC
1905
STEETONAFC
LOWER HOPTON
HOWDENS
DAMART

The FA Cup
sponsored by Budweiser
SILSDEN AFC
v.
ROSSINGTON MAIN
Saturday 20th August 2011 Kick off 3pm
AT THE ASDA FOUNDATION STADIUM
KEIGHLEY ROAD, SILSDEN BD20 0EH
R & R Builders
All types of work undertaken
Richard Feather
01535 656111
07754 606435
THOMAS CLARKSON
Contractors
01535 653262
Airevalley Independent Financial Advisers Ltd
MAIN SPONSOR:
ANGEL TELECOM Tel: 01274 758021

SILSDEN AFC
FOOTBALL'S COME HOME!
AFTER 7 YEARS!
CROOK TOWN FC
The FA CUP
e-on
THOMAS CLARKSON
01535 653262
THIS PRIME SPACE
COULD BE YOURS
FOR ONLY £60
PER SEASON
Jacksons
of Silsden
01535 652376
MAIN SPONSOR:
Angel Telecom
Tel: 01274 758021
angel

KEIGHLEY & DISTRICT RUGBY TEAMS

Keighley FC 1892/93

At the time, the team played in navy blue jerseys, with white shorts, and its headquarters was the Black Horse Hotel. In the summer of 1893 the club entered league competition for the first time, playing in the Yorkshire Intermediate Competition, effectively a third tier county league. At this time, 'Rugby' was still one sport, the Great Split not occurring until 1895.

Back: E Baldwin, T Parkinson, T Umpleby, J Howles. Second Row: J Blades, W H Helliwell, T McDonnell, A Slater, Abraham Naylor, R Blades, G Newhill. Third Row: W H Bastow, A Best, R Jennison, G Mitchell (Captain), J Crossley, D Bastow, A Sugden, Joseph Summerscales (President). Front: R Crossley, W Rundle.

Keighley & Keighley Juniors Fixtures 1883/84

KEIGHLEY F.C.

FIRST TEAM.
Oct. 6 Halifax St. Joseph's, h
13 Bradford Trinity, away
20 Hull Southcoates, home
27 Skipton, away
Nov. 3 Bradford Rangers, h
10 Bingley, away
17 Holbeck, away
24 Otley, home
Dec. 1 Shipley, away
8 Harrogate, home
15 Castleford, away
22 Halifax St. Joseph's, away
29 Dudley Hill, away
Jan. 5 Hull Southcoates, away
12 Skipton, home
19 Bradford Rangers, away
26 Shipley, home
Feb. 2 Harrogate, away
9 Holbeck, home
16 Otley, away
23 Bingley, home
Mar. 1 (Cup Tie), Hipperholme & Lightcliffe, away
15 Bradford Trinity, home
22 Castleford, home
29 Dudley Hill, home

A TEAM.
Halifax St. Joseph's away
Bradford Trinity, home
Leeds East End, away
Skipton, home
Bradford Rangers, away
Kirkstall St. Stephen's h
Holbeck, home
Otley, away
Shipley, home
Harrogate, away
Keighley Juniors, home
Halifax St. Joseph's, home
Dudley Hill, home
Leeds East End, home
Skipton away
Bradford Rangers, home
Shipley, away
Harrogate, home
Holbeck, home
Otley, home

Kirkstall St. Stephen's a

Bradford Trinity, away
Keighley Juniors, away
Dudley Hill, away

Hon. Secs.—Mr. H. WALL, Wellington Buildings, and Mr. H. B. SUMMERSCALES
Captains—1st, Mr. W. Yiend; 2nd, Mr. F. Rennie
Head-quarters and Dressing-room—Victoria Hotel
Ground—Dalton Lane, 5 minutes' walk from Keighley Station (Mid.)
Club Colours—Navy Blue and White Jersey, and Navy Blue Knickers and Hose

KEIGHLEY JUNIORS F.C.

Oct. 6 Opening Match, home
13 Bradford Rangers 2nd, away
20 Manningham Hornets, home
27 Leeds St. Andrew's, away
Nov. 3 Bradford St. Joseph's, away
10 Greengates, home
17 Otley 2nd, home
24 Great Horton 2nd, away
Dec. 1 Dewsbury Clarence, away
8 Leeds St. Andrew's, home
15 Keighley 2nd, away
22 Bingley (A team), away
29 Bradford Rangers 2nd, home
Jan. 5 Otley 2nd, away
12 Great Horton 2nd, home
19 Bradford St. Joseph's, home
26 Greengates, away
Feb. 2 Denholme, away
9 Bingley (A team), home
16 Manningham Hornets, away
23 Denholme, home
Mar. 1
8 Skipton 2nd, away
15 Dewsbury Clarence, home
22 Keighley 2nd, home
29 Skipton 2nd, home

Hon. Sec.—Mr. GEO. NEWHILL, 23, Lustre Street
Captain—Mr. R. WILKINSON
Head-quarters and Dressing-room—King's Head Hotel
Ground—Adjoining Holy Croft Board School, half-mile from Keighley Station (Mid.)
Club Colours—Black

Keighley FC 1899/1900

Keighley became champions of the Yorkshire Senior Competition for the first and final time in the 1899/1900 season. The team never defended its title as it jumped ship to the Northern Union (now known as Rugby League) in the summer of 1900 in order to retain an attractive fixture list against the county's better clubs.

Keighley NUFC 1920/21

Keighley RLFC 1937

Keighley has only once made the final of the Rugby League Challenge Cup. On that occasion the team lost 5-18 to Widnes at Wembley Stadium on 8th May 1937.

KEIGHLEY   WEMBLEY 1937.

Back Row   TOWILL   HALLIDAY   TALBOT   J. TRAILL   DIXON   JONES   SHERBURN   J GILL
Front Row   G. PARKER   LLOYD   D. M. DAVIES   BEVAN   HERBERT

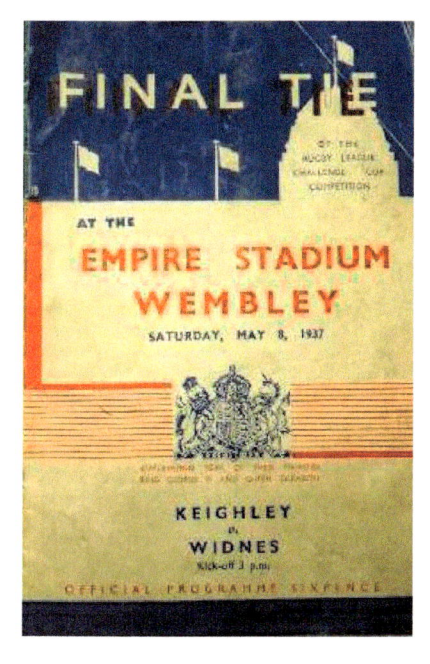

Challenge Cup Final Programme 1937 (left)

Top of the League 1938 (right)

A cartoon from the Keighley News celebrating the fact that the club was - albeit briefly - top of the Rugby League Championship during the 1938/39 season. It finished the season 13th of 28 teams,

Keighley RLFC 1937

This is the official Keighley Rugby League club team picture taken prior to their only appearance at Wembley in 1937. Published in the *Keighley News* on 1st May 1937. The picture was taken by Hall & Siggers, which was a partnership between Harry Hall and Frank Siggers who had worked together in Chelmsford, Essex. Looking for fresh fields from which to operate, the pair moved with their families up to Keighley in 1909. They bought up the studio of Keighley photographer Alexander Jennings at 105 Cavendish Street (Information from Eddie Kelly).

Worth Village Juniors

Medal competitions were common in the early 1900s, and were often organised by senior clubs in the town. Teams fielded players who had not played competitive rugby before, and they were popular end of season tournaments. Here we see Worth Village Juniors with their medals from the 1921 competition hosted by the senior Keighley club.

Keighley Hornets 1888/89

Keighley Hornets, formed in 1884, was a nomadic club playing on grounds at Thwaites, Bradford Road and Dalton Lane before folding late in 1892.

Keighley Zingari 1890s

This photograph is taken in either 1893 or 1894, when the team won the Keighley Charity Cup. The team played on a ground on Bradford Road, Stockbridge. It disbanded in 1896 but reformed in 1908, playing effectively as Keighley's 'A' team before folding for good during World War One.

Keighley Shamrocks 1894/95

Shamrocks were founded in 1885 at the town's Shamrock club at the bottom of Turkey Street. It was a somewhat nomadic club, but had moved into a ground on Calversyke Hill for the 1894/95 season. This coincided with the club's most successful season, when it won a remarkable 'treble'. The West Yorkshire League title was won following victory in a play-off with Dewsbury St Paulinus, and there were victories in the Keighley Charity Cup and Wharfedale Cup finals. Keighley Trinity was defeated 11-0 in the former, with Brownroyd Rec (Bradford) defeated 9-5 early in the season in the latter.

By the summer of 1898, however, Shamrocks had disbanded. The name has been revived a few times since then, albeit briefly, and has became associated with soccer rather than rugby in later years.

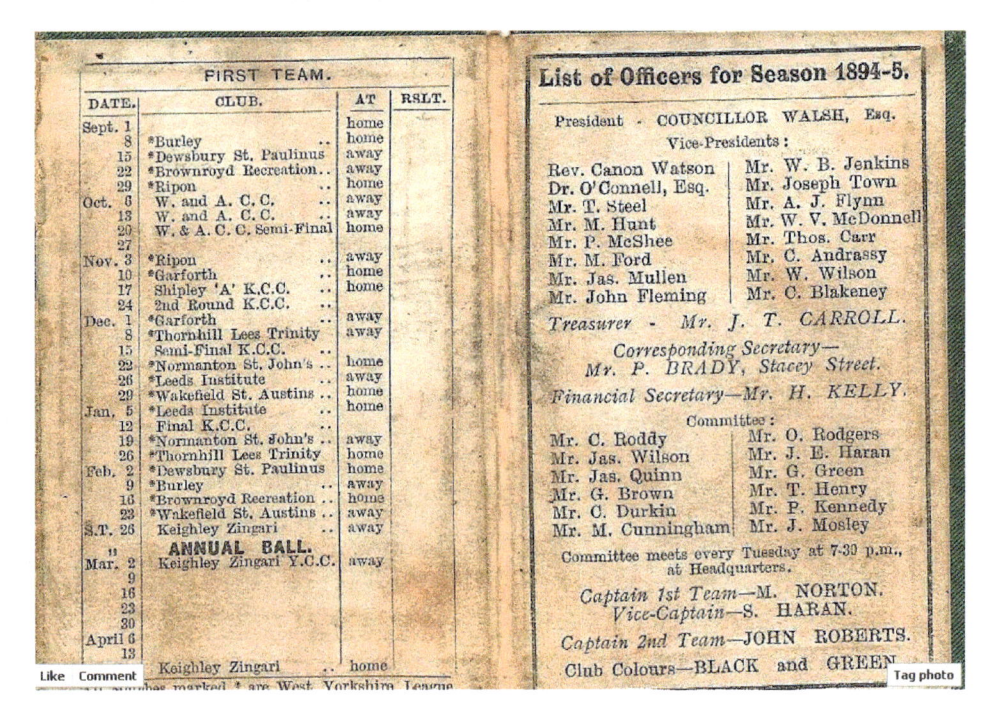

FIRST TEAM.

DATE.	CLUB.	AT	RSLT.
Sept. 1		home	
8	*Burley	home	
15	*Dewsbury St. Paulinus	away	
22	*Brownroyd Recreation	away	
29	*Ripon	home	
Oct. 6	W. and A. C. C.	away	
13	W. and A. C. C.	away	
20	W. & A. C. C. Semi-Final	home	
27			
Nov. 3	*Ripon	away	
10	*Garforth	home	
17	Shipley 'A' K.C.C.	home	
24	2nd Round K.C.C.		
Dec. 1	*Garforth	away	
8	*Thornhill Lees Trinity	away	
15	Semi-Final K.C.C.		
22	*Normanton St. John's	home	
26	*Leeds Institute	away	
29	*Wakefield St. Austins	home	
Jan. 5	*Leeds Institute	home	
12	Final K.C.C.		
19	*Normanton St. John's	away	
26	*Thornhill Lees Trinity	home	
Feb. 2	*Dewsbury St. Paulinus	home	
9	*Burley	away	
16	*Brownroyd Recreation	home	
23	*Wakefield St. Austins	away	
S.T. 26	Keighley Zingari	away	
"	ANNUAL BALL.		
Mar. 2	Keighley Zingari Y.C.C.	away	
9			
16			
23			
30			
April 6			
13			
	Keighley Zingari	home	

List of Officers for Season 1894-5.

President - COUNCILLOR WALSH, Esq.

Vice-Presidents:

Rev. Canon Watson	Mr. W. B. Jenkins
Dr. O'Connell, Esq.	Mr. Joseph Town
Mr. T. Steel	Mr. A. J. Flynn
Mr. M. Hunt	Mr. W. V. McDonnell
Mr. P. McShee	Mr. Thos. Carr
Mr. M. Ford	Mr. C. Andrassy
Mr. Jas. Mullen	Mr. W. Wilson
Mr. John Fleming	Mr. C. Blakeney

Treasurer - Mr. J. T. CARROLL.

Corresponding Secretary—
Mr. P. BRADY, Stacey Street.

Financial Secretary—Mr. H. KELLY.

Committee:

Mr. C. Roddy	Mr. O. Rodgers
Mr. Jas. Wilson	Mr. J. E. Haran
Mr. Jas. Quinn	Mr. G. Green
Mr. G. Brown	Mr. T. Henry
Mr. C. Durkin	Mr. P. Kennedy
Mr. M. Cunningham	Mr. J. Mosley

Committee meets every Tuesday at 7-30 p.m., at Headquarters.

Captain 1st Team—M. NORTON.
Vice-Captain—S. HARAN.

Captain 2nd Team—JOHN ROBERTS.

Club Colours—BLACK and GREEN

Haworth 1904/05

A first Haworth club played in the mid-1890s but the first really competitive club played between 1901-06. Here the team can be seen with the Keighley Charity Cup, which had been won the previous season when Keighley Olicana were defeated in the final. That was the last time that the competition would be run under Northern Union rugby rules (Courtesy of Steven Wood).

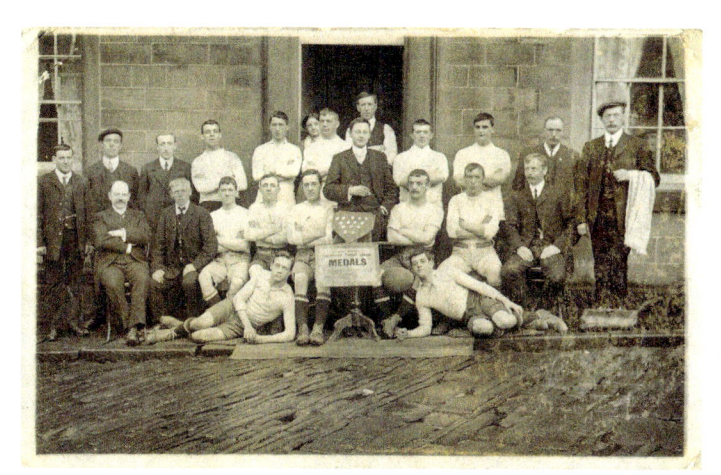

Haworth 1908/09

A revived Haworth club played for two seasons between 1908-10 in the Keighley Intermediate League. It is pictured here after winning the title in the first of those seasons. The league, and Haworth Northern Union club went into abeyance in the summer of 1910.

Oakworth Road Hornets 1925/26

This short-lived club played for just two seasons in the Keighley Intermediate League. Its players are photographed at the end its first season.

Back: Mr Whitran, J Meegan, B Cone, H Middleton, J Hugill, n/k, L McIntyre, A Frith. Middle: G Middleton, n/k, E Farrah, T Halligan, F Longley, D Pinder. Front: H Green, Ickringill.

Keighley RLFC Boys 1925/26

Northern Union was renamed as Rugby league in 1922, hence the term RLFC coming into use. This team played in the West Yorkshire Supporters League before joining the local Bradford and Keighley league competitions.

Keighley Highfield 1927/28

Formed by former Worth Village player Ayrton Anderton in 1926, this team at first played at Calversyke Hill (the former Shamrocks ground) before playing regular homes at Lawkholme Lane in 1931. Here the team is seen with both Keighley and Bradford Intermediate Trophies, which were won in the same season.

The team folded in 1937 although the 1933/34 season saw home games played in Haworth, so the team was called Haworth Highfield for that one season.

Back: the Middleton Brothers, Maiden, McGowan, Anderton, Mitchell. Middle: Stansfield, Riley, Whittaker, Robinson, Meekin, Jackson, Anderton (ballboy), Front: Coupland, Calvert, Holmes, Moore.

Dean Smith & Grace 1943/44

This team played in the Keighley Workshops Junior League in the 1943/44 season, winning that competition before spending a further season in the Huddersfield & District League.

Keighley Athletic 1945/46

This team was known as Keighley Boys and then Keighley Juniors (no relation to the previous club of that name) before being renamed Athletic in 1944. The side was renamed again, as Keighley Albion, in 1949.

Keighley Grammar School Rugby Union XV 1947/48

Rugby Union was still played in some schools, despite the dominance of Rugby League in the district.

Eastwood Tavern

The exact year this photo was taken is unknown, but the Eastwood Tavern team played between 1950-54, firstly on a ground at Utley, and then at the town's Greyhound Stadium. Playing in local league competitions, the team won the Keighley League in the 1951/52 season. When the team disbanded, most of its players moved on to play for Victoria Park Rangers, who shared the same ground. *Back: J Lowe, J Morley, E Newton, G Newton, unknown, H Metcalfe, B Emsley, R Hinson, F Fahy, J McKie, T Brooksbank. Front: H Slater, J Midgeley, G Brooksbank, B Middleton, F Moorby, J Caine, unknown, Robinson, Buckley.*

Keighlians RUFC

Formed as Keighley Old Boys in 1920, and later better known as Keighlians, the club has flown the flag for the 15-a-side game continuously since then. Taken in the 1930s, Thomas Frankland is sitting on the bottom row, third from left. (Courtesy of Helen Anstis).

Keighley RUFC 1947/48

The renamed Keighlians club marked its move to its new home at Thwaites by becoming the first team to win the Yorkshire Cup and Shield competitions in the same season Otley were defeated 14-9 in the Yorkshire Cup final at Skipton 17th April 1948. This has proved to be the club's only success in the county's premier competition to date.

Back: K Paver, N Carr, C Fearnside, D Pritchard, F Kidd, A Hirst. Middle: K Hudson, H Fennerty, K Pickles, A V Town, A Tillotson, N Judson, T H Fletcher, E Clapham, J McManus. Front: H Handley, G S Swift, J Hale, L Buckley, C Shackleton. Seated: J K Ramsden, J Smith

Left: The Yorkshire Cup

Right: The Yorkshire Shield

Keighlians & Keighley Boys' Grammar School Fixtures 1933/34

(Taken from the Yorkshire Rugby Union handbook for that season)

Keighley Albion 1954/55

The all conquering Albion team is seen here before its victory in the Bradford Cup final, which resulted in a resounding 28-0 win against Queensbury.

Three other trophies were won by Albion that season. Victoria Park Rangers were defeated in the Keighley Cup final, Ovenden defeated in a replay in the Halifax Cup final, and Silsden edged out 13-10 in a Keighley League decider at Strong Close.

Riddlesden 1948/49 & 1950/51

The original Riddlesden club played from 1895-1900 and actually switched to the Northern Union before the senior Keighley team did.

Left: The picture shows the revived club in its first season, 1948/49

Below left: A 1950-51 team group proudly displaying the Keighley Cup. This was the clubs' only success in local league & cup competition. Keighley Albion were edged out 9-7 in the final.

Victoria Park Rangers 1954/55 & 1958/59

Based at Keighley Greyhound Stadium, this club played between 1953-59 in local league competitions. The 1954/55 team was defeated in the Keighley Cup final by Keighley Albion (this photo was part of the Vine Tavern collection), while the 1958/59 team proved to be the club's last as the club folded that summer. One piece of silverware that was won was the Keighley League title in the 1957/58 season.

NSF Rangers 1963/64

The National Switch Factory's Rugby team first appeared late in the 1962/63 season. A change of name to Worth Village occurred early in the 1966/67 season. *Back: E Cowling (President), C Barrett, D Kent, A Bancroft, L Latta, D Browes, R Lund, S Kennedy, D Williamson, D Constantine (secretary), M Sharp. Front: D Feather, C Steele, R Ramsbottom, S Hebden, J Hartley, A Winterbottom, J Horn.*

Cartoons

Harry East was a regular scribe for *The Keighley News* in the late '50's & early '60's. Local sport did not escape his attention, and neither did the individuals featured here.

John Bradley, Silsden's scrum half.

Mr. K. I. Mason, manager, Keighley Lifts Rugby team.

Clive Rees, Victoria Park's full-back.

Barry Mitchell, Keighley Albion threequarter.

WATCH RUGBY LEAGUE FOOTBALL AT LAWKHOLME

THIS MATCH IS SPONSORED BY
SCOTT'S MOTOR SERVICES (Keighley) LTD and BRADFORD
Specialists in chauffeur-driven Limousine & Saloon Car Hire. Weddings, Executive Hire, Air, Sea and Rail Terminals. Coastal Resorts and Touring.
Write or telephone for brochures and tariff:
Keighley 2117 or 3678 and Bradford 493458.

SUNDAY, 5th JANUARY.   Kick-Off 3 p.m.
KEIGHLEY v. BRADFORD NORTHERN

SAT. 4th JANUARY, 1975
Kick-Off 3 p.m.
KEIGHLEY 'A' v. HULL KINGSTON ROVERS 'A'

12th JANUARY, 1975
KEIGHLEY v. ST. HELENS
Kick-Off 3 p.m.

Keighley RUFC 1981/82

The photograph is taken at the club's former ground at Marley.

Keighley Albion Under 17s 1980/81

Albion's under 17s proudly display their silverware for the 1980/81 season. Featured holding their trophies are captain P Knapper (left) and S Boocock (right) who missed all three finals with a broken wrist. Also in the picture are, *Back: G Tanner, Glen Palmer, T Williams, Andrew Preston, Gary Smith, A Karnasaukas, Dave Nixon, Paul Kit, Jeff Butterfield, S Clarke, Graham Gow. Front: A McGuire, G Kelly, Andrew Winterbottom, D Williamson (coach), Howard Packer, Warren Rockford* (Thanks to Andrew Winterbottom).

Keighley Albion 1980/81

Albion were playing second fiddle to Worth Village at this time, losing their fourth successive Tommy Holmes Cup final to their rivals in the 1980/81 season. They did win it for the first time the following season though. The Tommy Holmes Cup was basically a Keighley Cup competition.

Worth Village 1979/80

Village, along with Keighley Albion joined the newly created Pennine League in 1974. The team played in Division One (below the Premier Division), one division higher than Albion.

Oakworth Wanderers 1980/81

Formed by Allan Bancroft & David Ingham, Wanderers played in the Pennine League from 1980 to 1982, playing on the field adjacent to Oakworth Cricket Club. *Back:* D Ingham (manager), B Uttley (coach), N Haley, P Brierley, T Kendrick, L Robinson, J Spencer, M Barr, N Spencer, J Dickinson, G Bennett, G Bairstow (Chairman). *Front:* K Seaton, S Hewitt, J Ash, T Coffey, G Seward, J Rall, M Finn.

Keighley Star 1981/82

Photographed during their first season, the team played on until 1988 before folding. It had initially changed its name to Great Northern but folded before it had played a competitive fixture.

Keighley Albion 'A' 1984/85

Albion's second string reached the Halifax Supplementary Cup final, going down 8-22 to Boothtown at Thrum Hall. Neil Palmer and Simon Rix scored tries for Albion that day (Courtesy of Shaun Neil Kelly).

Keighley Albion Under 17s 1983/84 (Courtesy of Shaun Neil Kelly)

Silsden 1980/81 & 1982/83

Rugby League was revived in Cobbydale in 1979 after the previous club had been wound up in 1963. The teams early seasons saw it playing in the lower Divisions of the Pennine League.

Silsden 1986

The team is photographed after defeating rivals Rangers to retain the Silsden Shield in November 1986. The Shield was played between the two Silsden clubs between 1985-89, Silsden winning the first two matches, and Silsden Rangers the second two.

Silsden Rangers early 1990s

Formed as a breakaway from Silsden in 1984, the rival clubs joined together in 1992 to become Silsden Park Rangers (and then just Silsden in 2010).

Keighley Albion 1991/92

Tommy Holmes Cup winners this season, Silsden Rangers were defeated 22-11 in the final (Photo courtesy of Trevor Smith).

Worth Village 1992/93

Village regained the Tommy Holmes Cup with a resounding 36-4 victory against Keighley Albion in the final (Photo courtesy of Trevor Smith).

Worth Village, 7s winners 1996

Village defeated the hosts, Keighley Rugby Union Club, to win Celtic's pre-season 7's competition. *Team: J Lister, C Morphet, W McComb, J McComb, D Birkett, J Shaw, D Walton, G Baker, A Feather* (Photo courtesy of Trevor Smith).

Keighley Celtic 1992/93

Celtic ran from 1984 until its merger with Worth Village in 1999, playing in the Pennine League throughout. *Back: K Tretton, S Jowett, C Hannah, S Atkins, I Anderson, C Bell, S Revak, M Anderson, T Walsh, G Parker. Front: D Spencer, P Young, G Rankin, P Bastow, mascot R Spencer, P Walsh, H Parker, J McComb, B Shires.*

Keighley Celtic 1997/98

(Photo courtesy of Trevor Smith)

Worth Village 1997/98

Back: C Kelly, R Curtain, J Lister, D Walton, R Hellawell, J McComb, D Summerscales, D Atkinson, R Shaw, D Cox. Front: M Plunkett (Coach), D Birkett, J Shaw, W McComb, R McNulty, J Hollingsworth, B Davey, A Higgins, L Steadman (Photo courtesy of Trevor Smith).

Lawkholme Ladies 1985/86

The highly successful Lawkholme Ladies side of 1985-86. *Back: Karen Dunne, Victoria Hepworth, Heather Wilkinson, Julie Ellis, Helen Bailey, Senta Hepworth, Becky Vincent (manager), Middle: Mary Illingworth, Kathleen Peyton, Jayne Moses, Christine Hemsley, Jackie Spencer, Jane Thompson, Debbie Nixon, Front: Carolyn Armitage, Sarah Turner, Susan Thompson, Rhona Robinson, Angie Pickard, Michelle Redman.*

Keighley RUFC 2022

The photograph features the late Sam Walker, who is pictured with the ball. *Left to right top row: Nigel Curr, Mike Lewis, Ollie Sugden, Dean Brookes, Martin Curr, Stefan Mellor, Gregor Curr, Chris Morris, Harry Worstead, Joe Kaye, Nathan Berry, Matt Birkett, Billie Baker, Jake Hill, Liam Brookes. Bottom row: Andrew Marklew, Frank Ninniss – Fairbank, Jimmy Morton, Reece Somma, Allan Hobson – Sheriff, Sam Walker, Dave Pullan, Lee Watts, Arron Hands, Richard Simpson* (Courtesy of Kirsty Ambler).

Keighley RLFC programme covers through the years

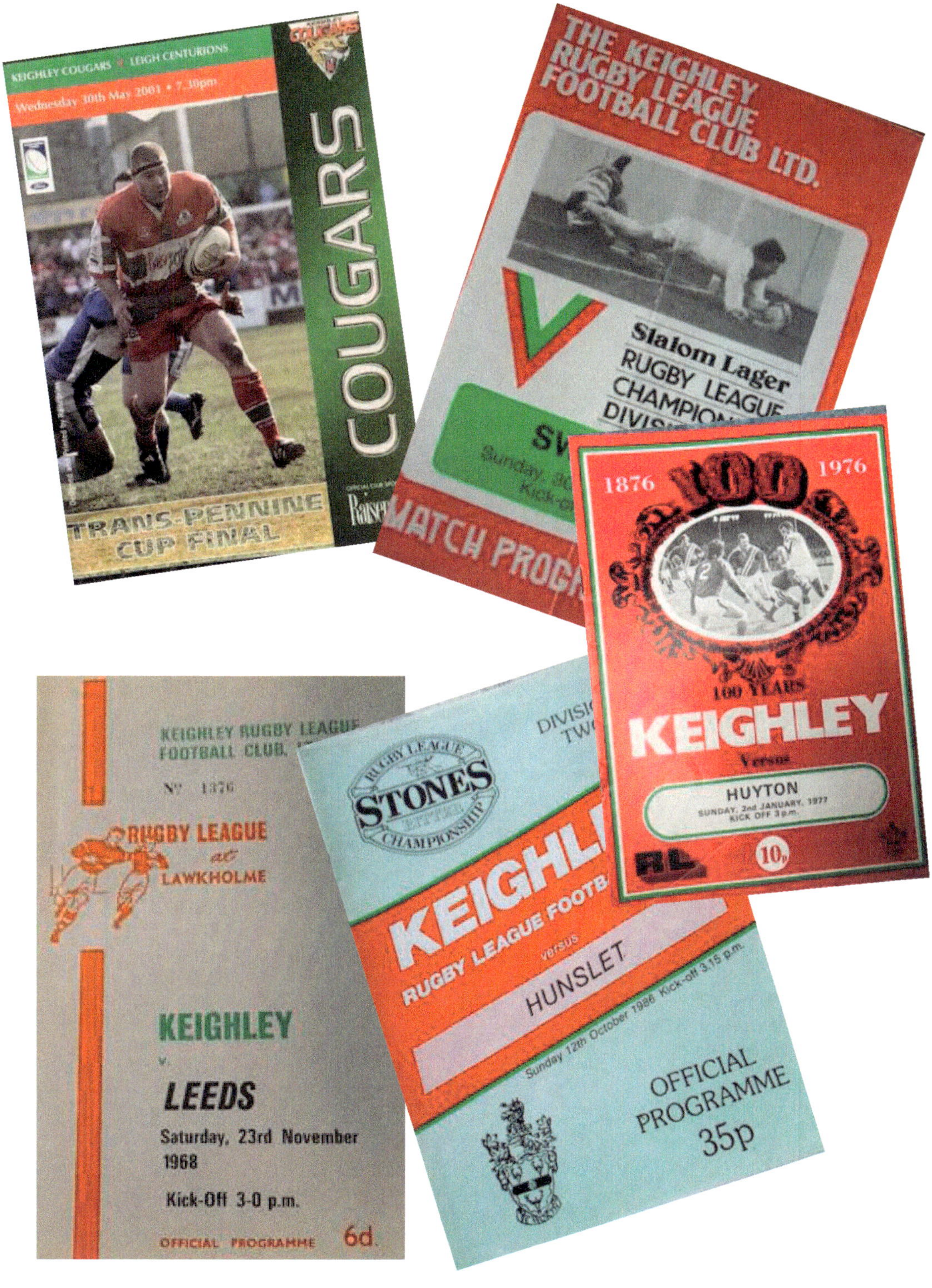
KEIGHLEY COUGARS v LEIGH CENTURIONS
Wednesday 30th May 2001 • 7.30pm
COUGARS
TRANS-PENNINE CUP FINAL
THE KEIGHLEY RUGBY LEAGUE FOOTBALL CLUB LTD.
Slalom Lager
RUGBY LEAGUE
CHAMPION
DIVIS
MATCH PROG
1876
1976
100 YEARS
KEIGHLEY
Versus
HUYTON
SUNDAY, 2nd JANUARY, 1977
KICK OFF 3 p.m.
10p
KEIGHLEY RUGBY LEAGUE FOOTBALL CLUB
Nº 1376
RUGBY LEAGUE at LAWKHOLME
KEIGHLEY
v.
LEEDS
Saturday, 23rd November 1968
Kick-Off 3-0 p.m.
OFFICIAL PROGRAMME
6d.
STONES
RUGBY LEAGUE
CHAMPIONSHIP
DIVISION TWO
KEIGHL
RUGBY LEAGUE FOOTB
versus
HUNSLET
Sunday 12th October 1986 Kick-off 3.15 p.m.
OFFICIAL PROGRAMME
35p

136

Keighley RUFC Programme Covers

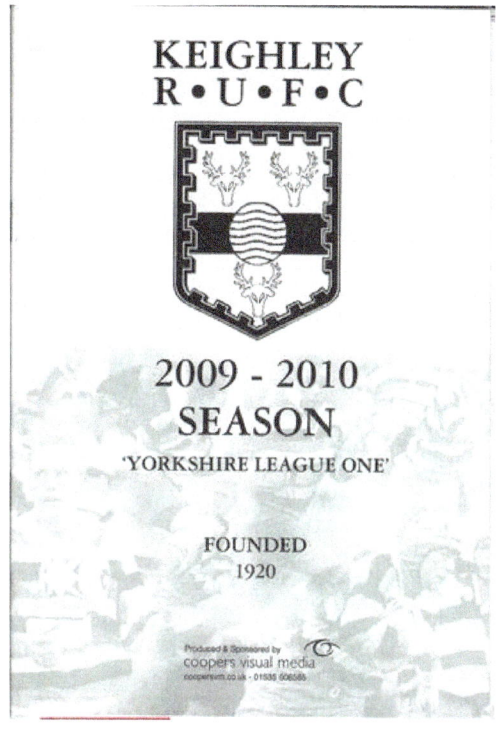

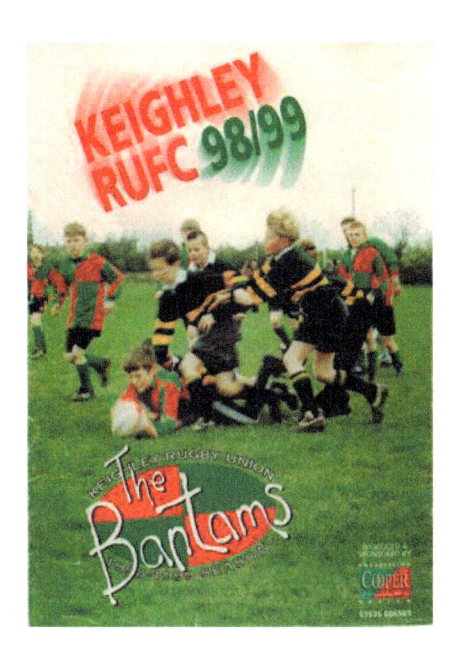

Keighley Albion ARLFC

KEIGHLEY & DISTRICT CRICKET TEAMS

Keighley 1865

The photograph from which the picture here is reproduced was sent to the *Keighley News* in 1925 from California. It was taken at Burnley on 22nd July 1865, a match which Keighley won, scoring 90 runs, to Burnley's 65. A Keighley Cricket Club can actually be traced back to 1848.

Back: J Dennison, W Luke Brown, J B Lund, n/k, Naylor (Umpire), Joseph Summerscales (captain), Ben Dean, J Braithwaite, Maude Scott. Front: W Greenwood, J Clapham, Tom Emmott. The boy on the front row was Joseph Rhodes who went on become a journalist.

Although Keighley Cricket Club originally played on a field on Dalton Lane, the doodles on this early scorecard suggests that matches may well have also taken place in the grounds of Eastwood House, which is now Victoria Park.

Clowns 1871

Exhibition matches attracted good crowds and raised funds for worthy causes. This match was played at Lawkholme Lane, a ground that Keighley Cricket Club had moved to just two years earlier. The advertisement and match report both come from *The Keighley News*.

DAN RICE'S GREAT CLOWN CRICKETERS.

Fourteen Professional CLOWNS in Costume will PLAY a MATCH on the KEIGHLEY CRICKET GROUND To-Day, against Eleven GENTLEMEN of the KEIGHLEY CLUB. Wickets pitched at Two o'clock.

The Clowns will Parade the town with the Band, starting from the Market Place at One o'clock.

CRICKET AND FUN COMBINED.

After the Match the Clowns will appear in their various performances on a stage erected in the Ground.

The Press is unanimous in praising the talent of each artiste, every one of them holding an eminent position in their profession.

Admission—4d. and 6d.

No Pass-out Checks, and no Change given at the gate.

ELEVEN OF KEIGHLEY v. FOURTEEN CLOWNS OF ENGLAND.—This match was played on the ground of the Keighley Club, in Lawkholme, on Saturday last, in the presence of a large number of spectators. From the annexed score it will be seen that Keighley won easily:—

KEIGHLEY.		THE CLOWNS.	
W. Widdop, c Batler b Myers	16	Fanny Franks, c Myers b Robinson	1
T. Jackson, c Boleno b Myers	12	Wheela, b Myers	2
R. Robinson, b Wallace	9	Myers, run out	8
J. Whitaker, c Myers b Wallace	13	Boleno, l b w b Robinson	4
R. Sedgwick, b Wallace	50	Wallace, c Widdop b Robinson	27
C. H. Foulds, c Myers b Wallace	11	Marteni, c Myers b Robinson	3
J. Scaife, c and b Myers	12	Batler, b Clough	0
W. Clough, st Myers b Wallace	34	Wellete, b Sedgwick	0
A. Smith, c and b Wallace	2	Maurice, not out	3
T. Myers, not out	10	C. Ricketts, run out	2
J. C. Wright, l b w b Wallace	7	De Lacy, c Widdop b Sedgwick	2
		H. Ricketts, c and b Sedgwick	0
		Deani, b Sedgwick	0
		H. Martani, b Sedgwick	0
Extras	3	Extras	7
Total	179	Total	59

St Peter's Fixtures Card 1888

The old St Peter's club represented the church of that name that was located on Halifax Road until it was demolished in 1956. The cricket club played friendly fixtures and then in local league competitions between 1874-97.

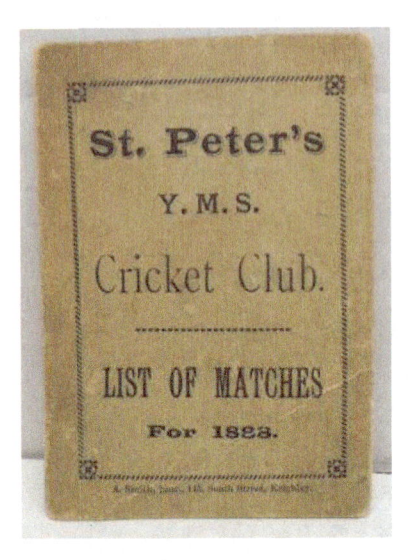

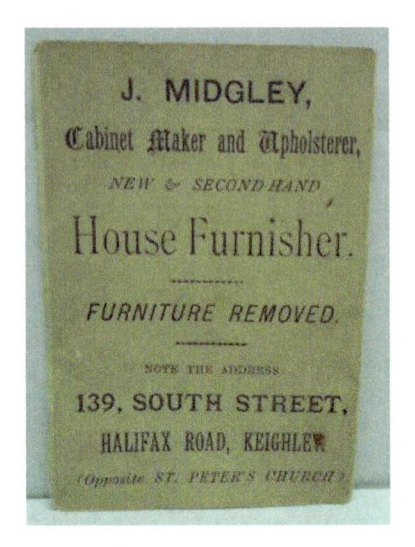

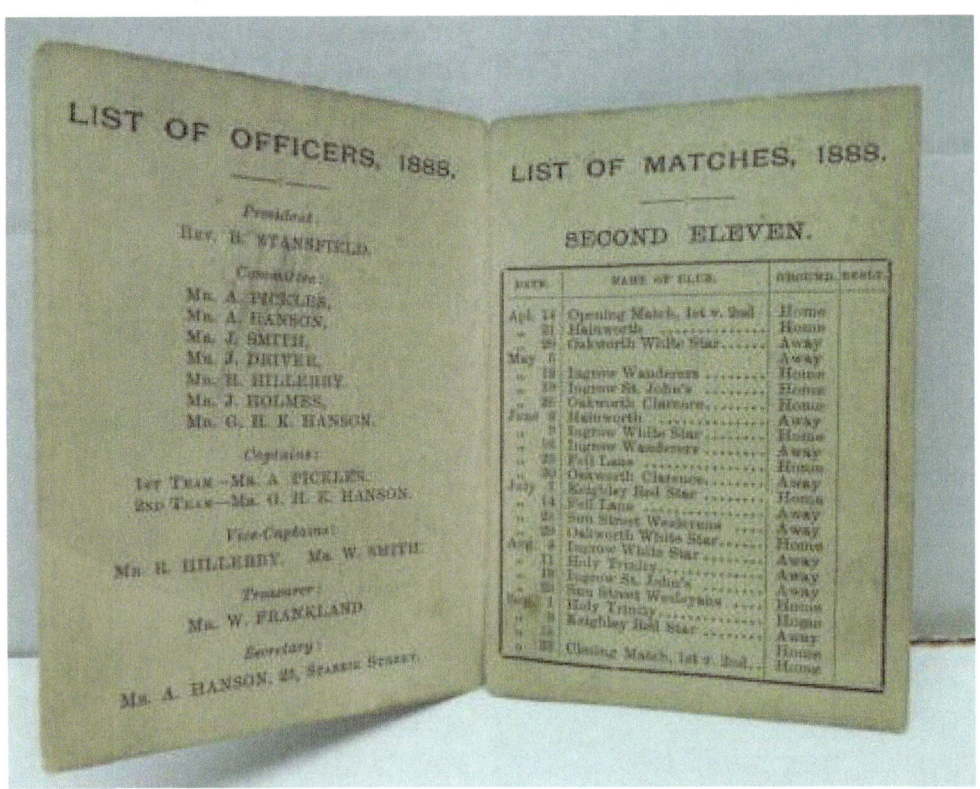

Ingrow St John's 1902

The first Ingrow St John's team played from 1879-1908 on a ground at the top of Occupation Lane. In 1902 the team defeated Horkingstone Baptists, which was a team from Oxenhope, to win the Keighley & District Sunday School League title. (Courtesy of Derek Newiss)

Haworth Wesleyans 1910

This is actually a photo of the club's second team, which won the Junior Division in the Keighley & District League. After a few name changes, the club is of course still in existence as Haworth CC.

Oxenhope Cricket Club Outing

The year this photograph was taken is unknown, but char-a-banc was a common means of travel in the early 1900s.

Silsden early 1900s

Founded in 1879, the club originally played at a ground on Sykes Lane when this photo was taken. The current ground at Keighley Road has only been in use since 1928.

Sutton Church 1911

The team won the Second Teams Competition in the Skipton & District League this season. Sutton and Kildwick Albion were the only first teams in the competition.

Kildwick Albion 1913

Two years after Sutton had done so, Kildwick Albion won the Second Teams Competition in the Skipton League. The team was in existence from 1892-1962.

Haworth Parish Church Second XI 1906

The Parish Church team was just pipped to the West Bradford League Second Teams title by Riddlesden in the 1906 season.

Haworth Baptists 1921

At this time there were three main Haworth clubs – Haworth Church (1894-1938), Haworth Wesleyans (the current Haworth CC), and the Baptists, founded in 1898, who were also variously known as Haworth West Lane and finally Haworth West End from 1970 until the club folded in 2015.

The Baptists' pavilion, on the hill top ground at Penistone Hill was built in 1921, and replaced in 1970.

However. One might note that there's a cup right at the front of the team. If that's the Keighley Cup then the photo is actually of Haworth Wesleyans, who won that competition in 1921

Keighley Boys Grammar School 1920s

Oxenhope Church 1925

Oxenhope Church played on grounds at Uppertown, Black Moor, and finally opposite the cemetery part way up Cock Hill. The photo above (courtesy of David Street) was taken in 1925, with the team displaying the Keighley & District League trophy and medals. The second photo shows the team with a slightly different trophy. The year is not known, and given that the Keighley League was also won in 1897, 1924, 1938, 1939 & 1946, and that the club's second team won the league's Junior division in 1921 it could be any of these years (except maybe 1897!).

In 1949 the club was reconstituted as Oxenhope Parish, and exists to this day albeit without the 'Parish' bit.

144

Fell Lane Second XI 1922

The Fell Lane club had just achieved the Keighley League 'double', with both first and second teams winning their respective divisions. However, three years later this successful local club had folded (Courtesy of Jeff Wallbank).

Cross Roads 1925

Cross Roads were Keighley Cup winners this season, defeating Long Lee in the final. The team also won the West Bradford League title, just ahead of Haworth Parish Church.

Parkwood Methodists

This team played on a ground at Parkwood Top and existed from 1896-1933 (Photo courtesy of Beverley Murray).

Oxenhope Wesleyans

The old Wesleyans club was founded in 1899 and played on a ground at Shaw Fields before locating to a ground on Dark lane, below Upper Hayley. It played on until 1939, when its team was replaced in the West Bradford League by the Oxenhope Church club.

Devonshire Street Congs fixtures 1928

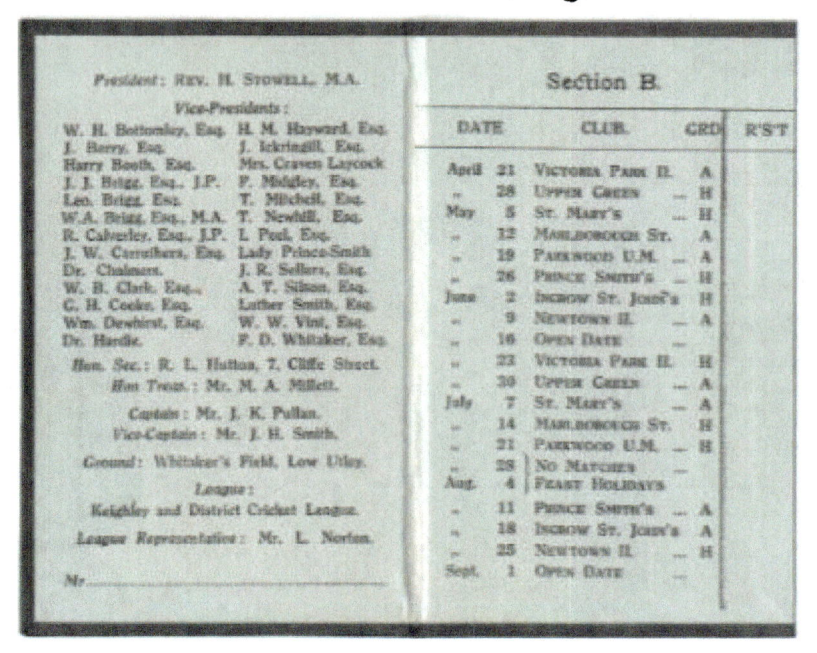

The Congs team was in existence for a good half century between 1912-62. During that time it played in the Keighley and West Bradford leagues.

Keighley Ladies 1930 & 1932

Keighley Cricket Club's Ladies team was active between at least 1929-54 and were champions of the Yorkshire Women's Federation in both 1932 and 1934 Despite experiencing much discrimination, incredulity and belittlement from those involved in the men's game, ladies cricket was particularly popular between the wars. Keighley Cricket Club itself ran a Ladies' League for local teams in at least 1949 (The 1932 photo is courtesy of John Bailey).

CAVENDISH HALL.

'AMERICAN ROLLER SKATING RINK.

STATION BRIDGE.   NOW OPEN.

THE FINEST RINK IN THE PROVINCES.

MILITARY BAND. EXPERT INSTRUCTORS (Lady and Gentlemen). SPLENDID PROMENADE. REFRESHMENTS.

MORNING, 10.30 to 12.30. Admission Free. Skates, 6d.

AFTERNOON, Two to Five—Admission, 3d.; Skates, 6d.; Ladies Free with Skate Tickets.

EVENING, Seven to Ten.—Monday, Tuesday, and Thursday.—Admission, Ladies, 3d.; Ladies free with skate ticket (6d.); Gents., 6d.; Skates, 6d. Wednesday, Friday, and Saturday, 6d.; Skates, 9d.

Saturday Nights, Open from Seven to 10.30.

LADIES' CRICKET MATCH ON SKATES.

KEIGHLEY LADIES versus ILKLEY LADIES,

THURSDAY NEXT, November 11th, at 8.30 p.m. Prompt.

ORDINARY SKATING BEFORE AND AFTER MATCH.

PRICES AS USUAL.   H. DAWSON, Manager.

Steeton 1931

Steeton were winners of the Wharfedale Section of the Yorkshire Council competition. At this time the club played on a ground close to Pot Lane, which has long since been built on.

Cross Roads 1931

The team finished runner-up to Crossflatts in the Keighley Cup in 1931.

From left to right: John Earnshaw, Frith Taylor, Norman Walmsley, n/k, John A Wood, Wilson, n/k, Herbert Hargreaves, John Smales, Percy Wheeler, Norman Daniels, Norman Smales.

Sydney Barnes

Perhaps the greatest cricketer to play for Keighley Cricket Club was the legendary Sydney Barnes (1873-1967). Before World War One he played 27 times for England, and in his final series in 1913-14 took a world record 49 wickets against South Africa. He played county cricket for Warwickshire and Lancashire as well as Minor Counties cricket for his native Staffordshire. After the War he played for Keighley's Bradford League rivals Saltaire between 1915-23 before playing league cricket in Lancashire. However, in 1934, aged 61, he returned to the Bradford League to play for Keighley, and this was his final season in league cricket before winding down his career.

Cross Roads

The year of each photo is unknown. The club's original ground was at Cragg Top, with those at Hardgate Lane (Sugden End) and Quarry House (Bingley Road) also being used in later years. A final move was made to the Brontë Playing Fields on Goose Cote Lane before the club moved out the Keighley district when it merged with Daisy Hill in November 2003.

Ingrow St John's 1934

After having struggled in the Keighley League, Ingrow St John's jumped ship to the Shipley & District League in 1934 and promptly carried off the league trophy in its first two seasons in that competition. *Back: N Welch (treasurer), P Hardacre (secretary), B Halliday, T Driver, C M Sharp, F Allsop, J Smith, Front: J Petit, J Whitaker, J R Scruton, Rev E N Pedley (President), G Greenwood, A Whitaker, J Brownbridge. Front: W Wellock, M Lindley, H Mitchell (Chairman), G Bown (Captain), W Cross (Vice Captain), A Shackleton, F Green.* (Courtesy of Derek Newiss)

Eastburn

The Eastburn team & officials are seen outside the old club pavilion on Lyon Road, year unknown.

Braithwaite St Matthew's

Photograph taken around 1940. The club originally played on a field at Calversyke but became established on another one just below Keighley Tarn. The club closed down in 1952, shortly after its pavilion was destroyed by fire. The church that the club represented is now known as Keighley New Church.

Riddlesden late 1930s

Riddlesden were West Bradford League champions in 1938, one year before local rivals Morton Banks (below) achieved that feat. The team won that league on no less than 12 more occasions. The club has played on its current ground since at least the 1890's, making it among the oldest continuously used sports grounds in the district. When founded in 1882, the club initially played on a field behind the Willow Tree Pub.

Morton Banks 1939

There had been previous Morton Banks teams before, but this incarnation was founded in 1920, initially playing on grounds close to Morton Banks Methodist Church and then Morton Banks Hospital. They moved to their ground at East Riddlesden Hall in 1936, three years before they won the West Bradford League title for the only time. The club folded in 1988, four years having been forced to leave the East Riddlesden Hall site.

MORTON BANKS CRICKET CLUB.
Winners of the West Bradford League Championship Cup Div. 1 Season 1939

Vale Mills Recs

Vale Mills played on a ground at East Royd, off Victoria Road, Oakworth. The team won the Keighley League in 1937, and then no fewer than eight times between 1951-60 before folding in 1966, so the undated photograph could show the winning team (& its silverware) from any of those years.

Keighley Sticker Club 1940

The formation of Keighley Sticker Club in 1940 was an attempt to raise the spirits of the local population during the war. Here Lancashire & Yorkshire cricketer Eddie Paynter, who played for Keighley at the time, is seen receiving his S-shaped badge, which cost just one penny.

Knowle Park Congs 1948

The club enjoyed a double success in 1948, winning the Keighley Cup for the second successive year as well as the West Bradford League Second Division title,

152

Knowle Park Congs 1950

The club ran from 1903 to 1973, and was at the height of its powers at this time, having lifted the Keighley Cup for the third time in four years. It had recently moved to its new ground at Crown Point, Occupation Lane in 1948. The Congs also finished as runner-up in the West Bradford League to Wilsden in 1950.

Cross Roads 1957

The club's first team won the West Bradford League's Second Division title in 1957, a feat that the club's Second Team also achieved in the same season.

Keighley Representative Team 1946

The team played in the Yorkshire Council Area Cup competition

Photographed are: F Sunderland (Scorer), F Buxton, A E Whittell, J Hargreaves, T Mawson, T Chatburn, G Halliday, J Reynold, B Greenwood, J Petyt, H Stirk, W Tatton, W Boardman (Captain), H Kirkley.

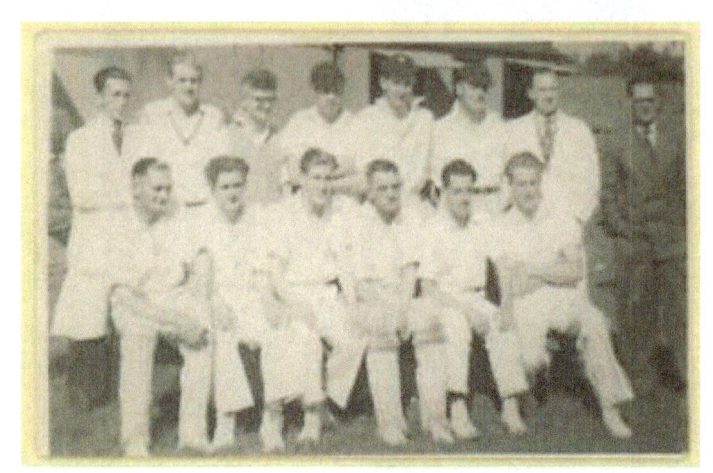

Keighley Lifts

An undated photograph of the team that played in the Keighley League between 1945-56, winning the title in 1952.

Keighley 1956

Twelve months earlier the club had finished rock bottom of the Bradford League's Second Division. 1956 was better, with a fourth from bottom finish. *Back: P Sunderland (Secretary), B Wilkinson, N S Hellawell, P Brook, A Goodwin, H Duffield. P J Anderton, C Cutter (League Rep.), K F Pattison. Front: G Spencer, P Gill (Vice Chairman), J W Tatton (Captain), L G Skirrow, W G McCarthy, J Emsley.*

Ingrow St John's 1959

If the year is correct, then this is the club's Second XI, which won the West Bradford League's Second Team competition.

Back: J H Greenwood (Scorer), T Overend, F Turbitt, H P Atkinson, E Britton, W H Lambert, A Ireton, J M Broadley, G S Dransfield, P Hardacre (Secretary). Front: S W Harrison, A Wood, Rev G Speller (President), B J Lindley (Captain), H R Mitchell (Chairman), H Hardacre (Vice Captain), B G Wood. (Courtesy of Derek Newiss)

Prince Smith & Stells

This photograph, possibly taken in 1958 contains the following players: *Back: Mel Bowman, Stanley Winchester, Norman Midgley, Alan Ackroyd, Robert Palmer. Front: John Cantwell, Norman Peers, Leo Bancroft, Harry Moore, Herbert Proctor.*

Long Lee 1963

The club had moved to Golden View in 1951 after having used a number of other grounds in the vicinity since the early 1900s. This photograph shows the opening of the new pavilion at Golden View.

Keighley Cricket Club 1961

The team is photographed with the league's Priestley Cup, which it had just won the fifth time. Note Mike Hellawell fourth from the left. The lifting of the cup was no mean feat for a club that was still stuck in the Bradford League's Second Division. It finished fifth in the division in 1961 and had to wait until 1965 to claim promotion back to the league's top flight.

There's only ONE shop in the district that's still 100% CYCLE SPECIALISTS and that's

HEATON'S
The Cycle Specialists
57 CAVENDISH STREET
KEIGHLEY
Phone 2727
PERSONAL ATTENTION AND 'ON THE SPOT' SERVICE
RESERVE YOUR JUNIOR CYCLE FOR XMAS NOW !

Dean Smith & Grace

The works' team played in local league competitions between 1949-68. The second photograph shows the team that had just broken Vale Mills Rec's monopoly on Keighley League titles.

1957 above: Back: A Winterbottom, n/k, K Wilkins, A Bailey, E Greenwood, A Wright, L Bell. Front: N Dodgson, E McDonald, F Buxton, n/k, n/k.

1961 left: Back: A Bailey, E Greenwood, A Wright, N Dodgson, E Holmes, R Senior. Front: N Pearce, K Stowell, F Buxton, E McDonald, J Clarke, K Parker.

Both photos were part of the Vine Tavern Collection.

Long Lee 1965

Back: Derek Granger, Billy Arnold, Alan Smith, John Greenwood, David Wilkinson, Tom Smith. Middle: Edgar Bottomley, David Baldwin, Roy Tetley, Brian Blowes, Jack Huggett. Front: Peter Huggett (Scorer)

Grange Middle School Under 11s National Softball Cricket Champions 1981

The team is photographed with teacher Rod Farnell (back centre). Middle: Simon White, Steven Lister, Jeremy Lumb, Michael Boulby, Michael Scarborough. Front: Jack Croft, Nigel Arnold, Andrew Addy, Duncan Ruckledge.

Grange Middle School Under 13s 1982

Back: Stuart Ruckledge, Andrew Addy, Mark Lister, Peter Dobson, Rod Farnell (Teacher), Jeremy Fay, Nigel Arnold, Mark Rankin, Christopher Cookson. Front: Simon White, Richard Hart, Steven Briggs, Michael Alvey, Daniel Belcher (Courtesy of Steven Briggs).

Morton Banks CC photographs (All courtesy of Eric Malcolm Binns)

Left: Sir Len Hutton presents a prize in October 1949

Right, year unknown

Left, around 1960

Right, 1971

Keighley Cup winners for the first and only time in the club's history. Cullingworth were the defeated team that year.

Left, year unknown

'*This photo features two interesting characters. T Barrett who lived at Barley Cote and became I think a squadron leader and flew Hunter jets . I can remember him doing a like bombing run over his house and tipping his wings as he flew low over . The other guy is a guy called Towler who arranged the Riddlesden Gala. Les Townsend was the captain*' (Words by Eric Malcolm Binns).

1972 Binns feat,

Malcolm Binns played for Morton Banks, Oxenhope and Oakworth. He also took 9 for 9 in a West Bradford junior League match (Courtesy of Eric Malcolm Binns)

Oakworth 1973

The photo is from the Vine Tavern Collection. At that time Oakworth were in the second tier of the West Bradford League.

Back: B Pennington, C Greenwood, A Brooks, S Broadbent, J Hobson, Barry Sayer, J Blackburn (Scorer), Jack Scarborough. Front: R Harris, D Greenwood, D Bottomley, W Scarborough, T Conway.

Ingrow St John's 1984 & 1995

The 1984 photo shows the team that was playing in the top division of the Dales Council League. The 1995 team played in the top division of the Craven League (Both photos courtesy of Derek Newiss).

Haworth West End Pavilion

One of the highest cricket pitches in the country, on top of Penistone Hill, Haworth West End used the ground from 1906 until it folded in 2015. It was used by other clubs for a short while after that but it is sadly no longer used for cricket.

RACE WALKING

A photograph, probably taken in the early 1900s , said to show the start of a walking event at Worth Village Gala. It could also be the start of a running event.

THE RUNNERS

Ingrow Harriers 1896/97

The photograph is taken in Lund Park, and contains a veritable who's-who of Keighley distance running of the time. Founded in 1894, the club was obviously thriving by the time the photograph was taken. It merged with another local club in 1898 and changed its name to Keighley Harriers in 1903. Within a couple of years of that name change the club seems to have faded away, however.

Back row: S Moore, F Taylor. H Rhodes, J B Carr (hon. secretary), R Bennett, W Jones, E Ascough, T H Knight, W F Scott, E Cawthron,
Middle row: Alf Smith, A Spencer, J Clayton, H Sanderson, H Robinson, J Dray, R J Whittaker, H Mather, E Smith, F Hardy, M Spencer, J Boast (trainer), A Morgan,
Front row: H A Gee, W Hobson, T Holmes, G H Atkinson, B Thornton, Harry Binns, J Fenlan, J Kurney, W E Bygrave, J Wright,
Sat/lying: W Clough, T Caulfield, A Hobson.

Fixture Lists

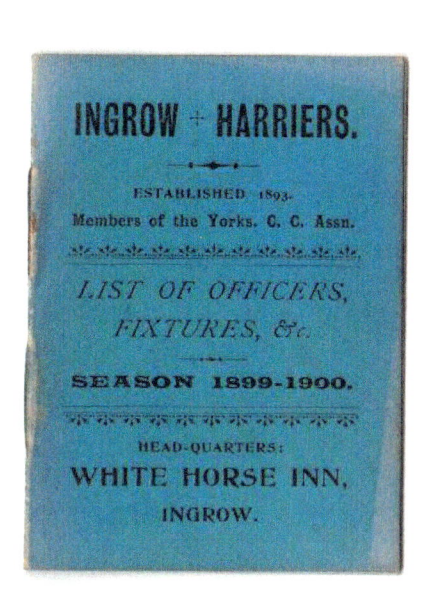

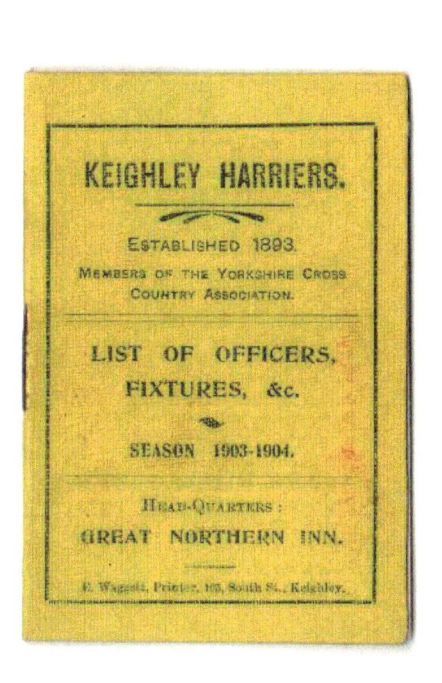

List of Fixtures, 1899.

Date	Event	Time of Starting
Sept. 30.—	Headquarters: Invitation Run.	3-30
Oct. 7.—	Headquarters.	3-30
,, 14.—	Headquarters.	3-30
,, 21.—	Keighley: Globe Inn.	3-30
,, 28.—	Bingley: Inter-run Bingley Harriers. Train 2-36.	3-15
Nov. 4.—	Headquarters: Inter-run Bradford Harriers.	3-15
,, 11.—	Bocking: New Inn.	3-30
,, 18.—	Headquarters.	3-15
,, 25.—	*Headquarters: FOUR MILES NOVICE HANDICAP. (Hebden Bridge Road Course)	3-30
Dec. 2.—	Laisterdyke: Inter-run Laisterdyke H. Train 2-25.	3-30
,, 9.—	Keighley: Bolt Makers Arms.	3-15
,, 16.—	Headquarters: Inter-run Skipton Parish Church H.	3-15
,, 23.—	†Headquarters: SIX MILES HANDICAP. (Hebden Bridge Road Course). Tea and Social after Race.	3-30
,, 30.—	Ingrow: Worth Valley Hotel.	3-15

*Four Runs to qualify.   †Five Runs to qualify.

List of Fixtures, 1900.

Date	Event	Time of Starting
Jan. 6.—	Headquarters: Inter-run Bingley Harriers.	3-15
,, 13.—	Keighley: Bridge Inn.	3-0
,, 20.—	Frizinghall: Turf Tavern: Inter-run Bradford Harriers. Train 2-36.	3-15
,, 27.—	Headquarters: Inter-run Laisterdyke Harriers.	3-15
Feb. 3.—	Headquarters: EIGHT MILES CLUB CHAMPIONSHIP. (Denholme and back Course).	3-30
,, 10.—	Ingrow: Great Northern Inn.	3-15
,, 17.—	Skipton: Inter-run Skipton Parish Church H. Train 2-35.	3-10
,, 24.—	Thwaites: Shoulder of Mutton Inn.	3-20
Mar. 3.—	Headquarters.	3-15
,, 10.—	Y.C.C.A. CHAMPIONSHIPS.	
,, 17.—	Keighley: Bolt Makers Arms.	3-30
,, 24.—	‡Headquarters: FOUR MILES HANDICAP. (Skipton Road Course).	3-30

‡Ten Runs to qualify.

LIST OF FIXTURES, 1903.

Date	Event	Time of Starting
Oct. 10—	Ingrow: Great Northern Inn	3-30
,, 17—	Wilsden: Inter-run Wilsden Harriers	3-30
,, 24—	Thwaites: Shoulder of Mutton	3-30
,, 31—	Keighley: Haymarket Hotel	3-30
Nov. 7—	Ingrow: Great Northern Inn	3-15
,, 14—	Keighley: Cricketers' Arms	3-15
,, 21—	Keighley: Angel Inn	3-15
,, 28—	Ingrow: ‡ 4 Miles Handicap	3-30
Dec. 5—	Keighley: Brunswick Arms	3-15
,, 12—	Sutton: Bay Horse Inn	3-30
,, 19—	Thwaites: Shoulder of Mutton, Inter-run Bingley Harriers	3-30
,, 26—	Ingrow: Great Northern Inn, Inter-run Wilsden Harriers	

‡ 4 runs to qualify.

LIST OF FIXTURES, 1904.

Date	Event	Time of Starting
Jan. 2—	Bingley: Inter-run Bingley Harriers	3-30
,, 9—	Keighley: Brunswick Arms	3-15
,, 16—	Thwaites: Shoulder of Mutton	3-15
,, 23—	Keighley: Cricketers' Arms	3-15
,, 30—	Ingrow: * 6 Miles Handicap	3-30
Feb. 6—	Bocking: Railway Inn	3-30
,, 13—	Ingrow: Great Northern Inn	3-30
,, 20—	Silsden	3-30
,, 27—	Wilsden: Inter-run Wilsden Harriers	3-30
Mar. 5—	Keighley: Haymarket Hotel, Inter-run Wilsden Harriers	3-30
,, 12—	Yorkshire C.C.A. Championship	
,, 19—	Open: See Notice	
,, 26—	Ingrow: † 8 Miles Club Championship	

* 8 runs to qualify.   † Any Member may run.

INGROW HARRIERS.

ESTABLISHED 1893.
Members of the Yorks. C. C. Assn.

LIST OF OFFICERS, FIXTURES, &c.

SEASON 1899-1900.

HEAD-QUARTERS:
WHITE HORSE INN,
INGROW.

KEIGHLEY HARRIERS.

ESTABLISHED 1893.
MEMBERS OF THE YORKSHIRE CROSS COUNTRY ASSOCIATION.

LIST OF OFFICERS, FIXTURES, &c.

SEASON 1903-1904.

HEAD-QUARTERS:
GREAT NORTHERN INN.

E. Waggett, Printer, 105, South St., Keighley.

Keighley Harriers 1912/13

A new Keighley Harriers was up and running between 1910-29. The appeal in the club handbook is interesting as cross country runners had a tendency to make themselves unpopular with local farmers, due to damage done to walls and hedges, that on top of the litter that was left during paper chases.

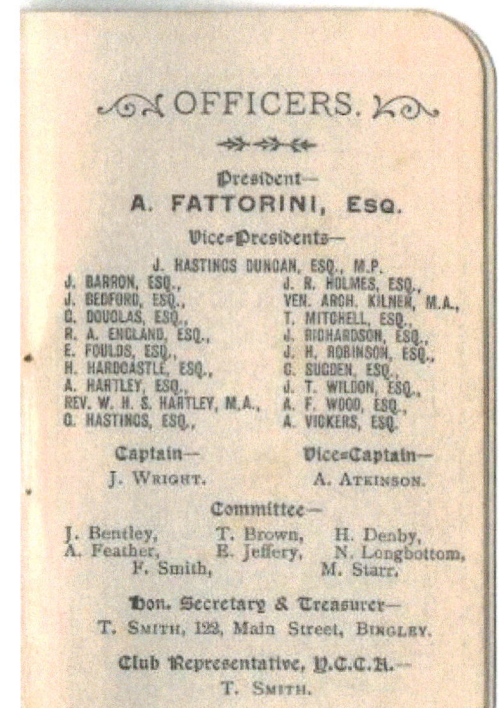

OFFICERS.

President—
A. FATTORINI, ESQ.

Vice-Presidents—
J. HASTINGS DUNCAN, ESQ., M.P.
J. BARRON, ESQ.,
J. BEDFORD, ESQ.,
C. DOUGLAS, ESQ.,
R. A. ENGLAND, ESQ.,
E. FOULDS, ESQ.,
H. HARDCASTLE, ESQ.,
A. HARTLEY, ESQ.,
REV. W. H. S. HARTLEY, M.A.,
C. HASTINGS, ESQ.,
J. R. HOLMES, ESQ.,
VEN. ARCH. KILNER, M.A.,
T. MITCHELL, ESQ.,
J. RICHARDSON, ESQ.,
J. H. ROBINSON, ESQ.,
C. SUGDEN, ESQ.,
J. T. WILDON, ESQ.,
A. F. WOOD, ESQ.,
A. VICKERS, ESQ.

Captain—
J. WRIGHT.

Vice-Captain—
A. ATKINSON.

Committee—
J. Bentley, T. Brown, H. Denby,
A. Feather, E. Jeffery, N. Longbottom,
F. Smith, M. Starr.

Hon. Secretary & Treasurer—
T. SMITH, 122, Main Street, BINGLEY.

Club Representative, Y.C.C.R.—
T. SMITH.

CLUB NOTICES.

The definition of a Novice to be as follows:
A Novice to be a runner who as never won a prize in a mile or over a mile.
(Bradford and District Junior definition.)

One attendance Prize will be given to the member making most attendances at weekly runs throughout the season.

Members of Football Clubs and other Harrier Clubs may train with Keighley and District Harriers on payment of 1/- for season 1912-13.

Notices will be posted in Mr. W. Moore's window 12, High Street.

The Committee hope members will endeavour to induce as many new runners to join the club as possible and also unite in making the visits of clubs successful.

AN APPEAL.

Members are requested when taking part in any club run, to conduct themselves as orderly as possible, and to use reason and care when crossing over walls and fences, so as not to damage them in any way. As Cross Country Running is only allowed on sufferance it is earnestly hoped that members will not abuse the privilege and so bring the sport into dis-repute.

1912.—Training Nights—Tuesdays from Headquarters at 7-30.

1913.—Tuesdays & Thursdays from Headquarters at 7-30.

Hares dispatched each Saturday, wet or fine.

Keighley Harriers 1912

The team is featured with the Bradford & District Cross County Championship shield after winning the junior team title at Clock House playing fields, Bradford. John Petty won the race – run over a 10 lap, 5 mile course – and he was backed up by H Wright (5th), B Driver (11th), H Wimblett (19th) & F Leighton (23rd). John Petty was the father of professional cyclist Doug Petty, who also features in this book. (Photos courtesy of Liz Spencer Petty).

A selection of medals from John Petty's collection

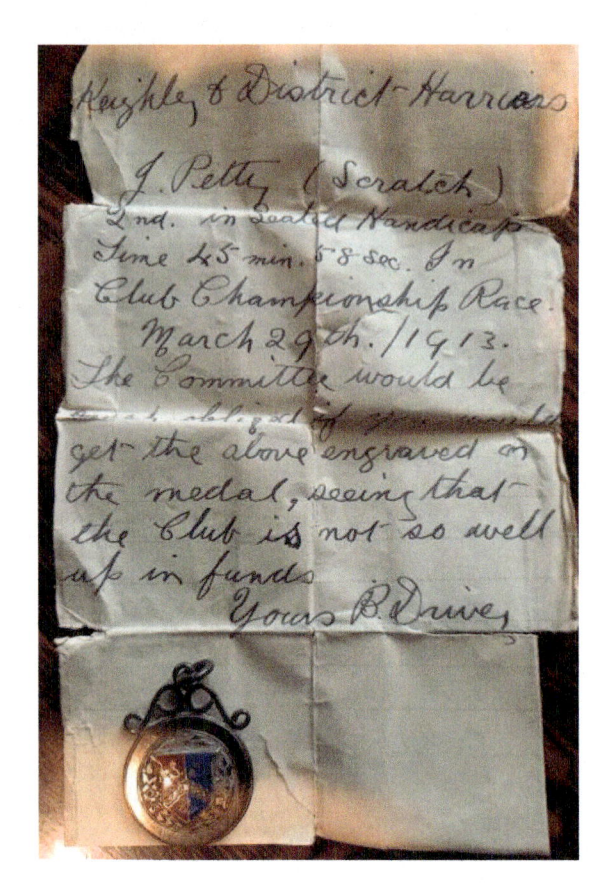

166

Harriers v Cyclists 1928

Photographed at the start line on Cooke Lane are members of Keighley Harriers and Keighley Road Club, which had been founded four years earlier. All of the runners finished before the first cyclist, suggesting that the route via Devonshire Street, Briggs' Fields, Fell Lane, Oakworth, Newsholme, Goose Eye, Keighley Tarn, Devonshire Park, and back to the start, was definitely one that suited those on two feet rather than two wheels.

A FAMOUS MILER

Derek Ibbotson completing the last lap of the mile race at the Yorkshire Athletics Championships at Marley Stadium, Keighley, on Saturday. Ibbotson won with a time of 4 min. 10.5 sec.

Derek Ibbotson's appearance at Marley in July 1957 no doubt helped to swell the attendance to 2,000 for the County Athletics Championships. The Olympic Bronze medallist over 5,000 metres would later in the year break the world mile record.

Taken from the Keighley Boys' Grammar School Magazine in Summer 1950, the winners of the one mile cross country race are featured here (Courtesy of Keighley Local History Society)

WINNERS 1 MILE (Open)
left to right, T. M. Driver (3rd), R. Clarke (1st), E. C. Pickering (2nd)

Oakbank churned out some top quality runners in the late 1970s and early 1980s. Here we see Steve Binns, Paul Denby, Colin Moore, and Robert Wayte, pictured in 1979.

Keighley Girls' Grammar School Sports Team 1942

(Courtesy of Keighley Local History Society)

Highfield School Athletics Teams

1953

(Courtesy of Keighley Local History Society)

1963

(Courtesy of Keighley Local History Society)

1964

Eventual winner Richard Lamb (87) leads future winner Mick Hawkins (67) and past winner Keith Summersgill (122) at the start of the 1983 Keighley RUFC Half Marathon

Dave Throup is flanked by Stephen Hill (102) and Dave Woodhead following the Silsden Five mile Road Race in 1985.

Eventual winner Mark Benson (Leeds City, 429) tracks team-mate P Jones (385) in the Budge 10K, run on the Aire Valley road between Kildwick & Utley just a week before the road was opened to traffic in April 1998. Runner-up Pete Moon is partially hidden behind the leaders. Steven Hill (who finished fifth) is seen in white, while fourth placed Chris Proctor is completely hidden. Sean Winstanley came through to finish in third place. The top 5 runners to finish were all well inside 31 minutes.

Eventual winner Mick Hawkins (number 5) leads the pack in the inaugural Keighley Town Centre 10K in August 1986. Just to his left are Chris Proctor and Stephen Hill (number 4). Hawkins won in 30 mins, 51 secs. World Veteran's Champion Derrick Lawson is at the back of the bunch (Photo courtesy of Peter Carr).

Dave Throup leads out the runners at the start of the Keighley 10K in 1990. Race winner Tony Okell (Stockport) is just to the right of runner 121. Runner up, Graham Ellis (Holmfirth) is obscured third from left. Number 113 came third. He writes books. Future Inter Counties 20-mile champion Shaun Winstanley is in the centre of the photo in the familiar hoops of Bingley Harriers.

Keighley's Steve Brooks (Bingley Harriers) leads the Ethiopians in Keighley's fastest ever 10K race in 1992. It was won in 29 minutes dead, the top four all finishing within four seconds of each other. Brooks finished 7th in 30.08. Colin Moore (who finished 8th) leads the chasing bunch.

Auld Lang Syne Fell Race 2008

It might look very cold and very foggy up at the start on Penistone Hill. It was. Perfect fell running weather. (Courtesy of Dave & Eileen Woodhead)

Keighley & Craven Ladies' team, silver medallists in the 1998 English Fell Running championship. From left to right are Freda Tate, Liz Tomes, and Jo Prowse (who won the Yorkshire 10 mile title on the road the following year). They are flanked by guests of honour Colin Donnelly, and Sarah Rowell at the Fell Runner's Association presentation evening.

Dave Slater was born in Keighley before moving to Baildon and achieving international success with Bingley Harriers. Here he is seen taking over from Pete Moon - a long time Keighley resident - in the 1977 Northern 6-stage road relay in Wakefield (Courtesy of Peter Moon)

The Keighley 10K & 5K races, in aid of the Sue Ryder Manorlands Hospice, are a popular event on the race calendar. Here runners are seen heading out into the rain at the start of the 2024 10K. Keighley's Callum James, the eventual runner-up, tracks race winner Jack Cummings (Ilkley Harriers).

More Keighley & Craven AC Vests

Top left: **Helen Glover** (now Helen Smith), an England international, celebrates her fourth victory in the Stanbury Splash Fell race in January 2014

Top right: **Sarah O'Sullivan** leads a bunch at the Bronte 5 mile road race in June 2022

Bottom left: **Hinda Hardacre** en route to winning the Littondale 4 Mile Road Race in 2019. Team-mate **Shaun Wilkinson** is close behind

Bottom right: **Lorna Hubbard** braving the rain in the 2024 Keighley 10K

(All four photographs courtesy of Dave & Eileen Woodhead)

Other well known local runners

From left: **Stewart McDonald**, a member of the Bingley cross country team that won the National title in 1991 & 1993, seen in action at the Bronte 5 mile road race around Haworth. Another popular runner, **Paul Crabtree**, also at the Bronte 5. **Chris Proctor**. His untimely death in 1998 led to his employers, Ashley Forge, donating the *Chris Proctor Trophy* to Keighley & Craven AC, and it is awarded annually to the winner of the club's road championship. (Photos of McDonald & Crabtree courtesy of Dave & Eileen Woodhead)

Below, K&C junior coach **Matt House** out on the fells, and **Emma Raven** (right), who won a bronze medal in the 1500m at the British Masters Track and Field Champs in Derby in July 2024 (courtesy of K&C). Bottom right is **Tim Clegg**, originally a member of Keighley Road Runners who is still turning out regularly for K&C some four decades later (Courtesy of Dave & Eileen Woodhead)

Oakworth Road Runners 2023

Club members are seen at the Bolton Abbey Summer Solstice Race. The club is run by fitness instructor, personal trainer, and running coach Beth Brunskill (Photo courtesy of Beth Brunskill).

Haworth Social Runners 2023

Haworth Social Runners, run by Lee Hamblin and Sarah Ogden, is a casual social trail running group. Here its members pose before the Yorkshireman Marathon (Courtesy of Lee Hamblin).

Wharfedale Harriers

Wharfedale Harriers, based in Silsden, has been a highly successful club since its inception in 1998, particularly on the fells. It's men's team were also winners of the West Yorkshire Cross Country League in 2018, its team consisting of Ali Burns, Robin Howie, Ethan Hassel, Christian Holmes, Tom Millard, Paul Crabby Crabtree, Adam Stirk, Jonny Bradshaw, and Ted Mason as team scorers at the races and with the likes of Dave McGuire, Dave Kirkham, Sam Watson, Chris Jones and Geoff Thompson backing them up (Courtesy of Wharfedale Harriers).

Wharfedale's **Emma Hopkinson** has been successful, particularly on the fells since the 1990s. **Tom Hooper i**s seen here destroying the opposition in the 2024 Silsden Murder Mile (Courtesy of Wharfedale Harriers).

parkrun

parkrun (with a small 'p') has come a long way since the first ever Bushy Park time trial in London in October 2004, with more than 2,300 weekly 5 kilometre events now taking place across not only the UK, but many other parts of the world. Carol & David Senior set up the Cliffe Castle Park run in 2018, the first being on 15th September of that year. The weekly, timed event has – at the time of publication – attracted over 7,000 runners of all ages and abilities to the park each Saturday morning at 9am. Philip Bland is often on hand with his camera, and these are all from his collection.

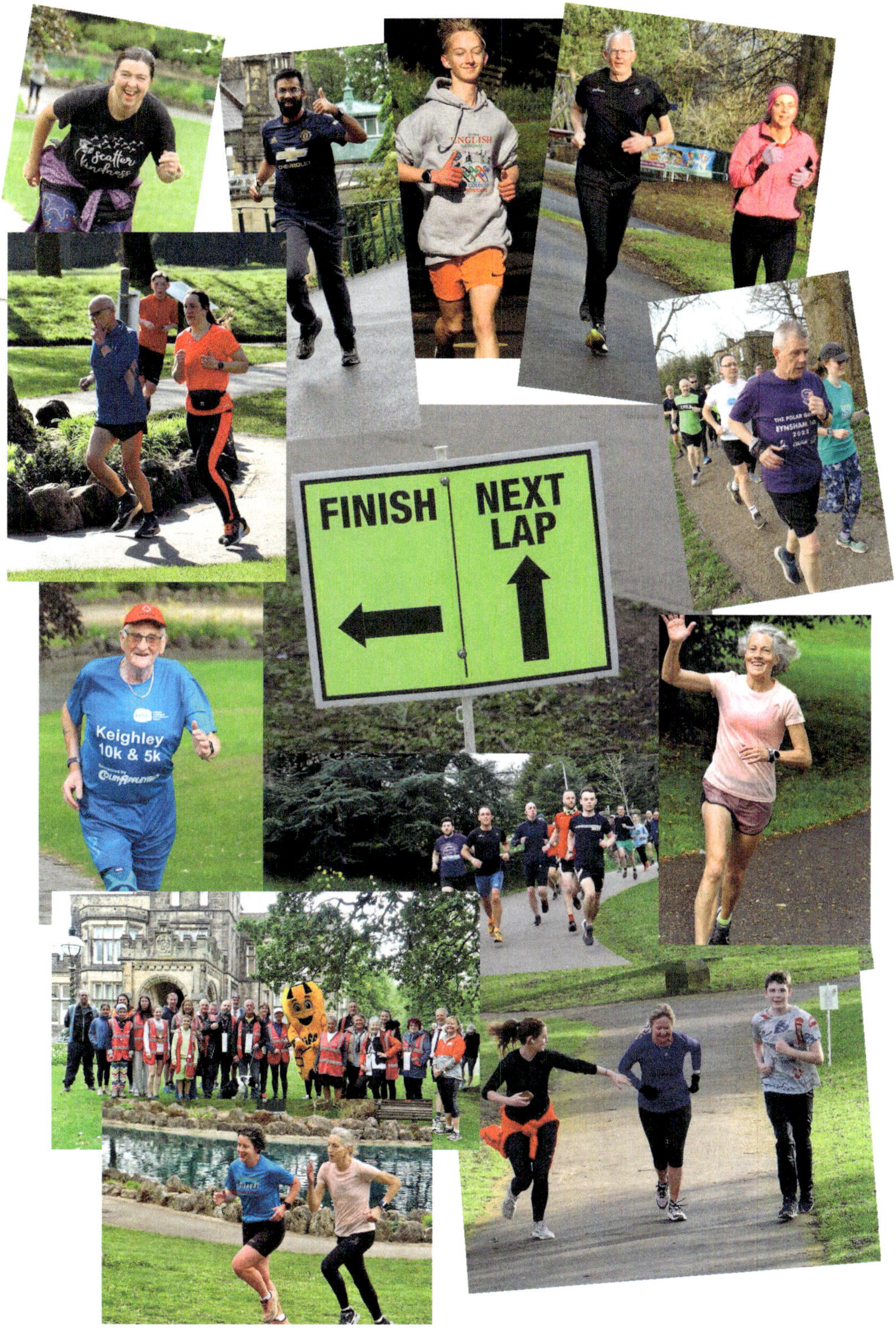
FINISH
NEXT
LAP
Keighley
10k & 5k

PASS THIS POINT
THREE TIMES
BEFORE GOING
TO THE FINISH

FINISH

THE BOXERS

Arthur Barnes (who is in the top right photograph) headed the bill at the event promoted by Sam Scaife. The result was a draw but Barnes won his re-match with Jarvis soon after.

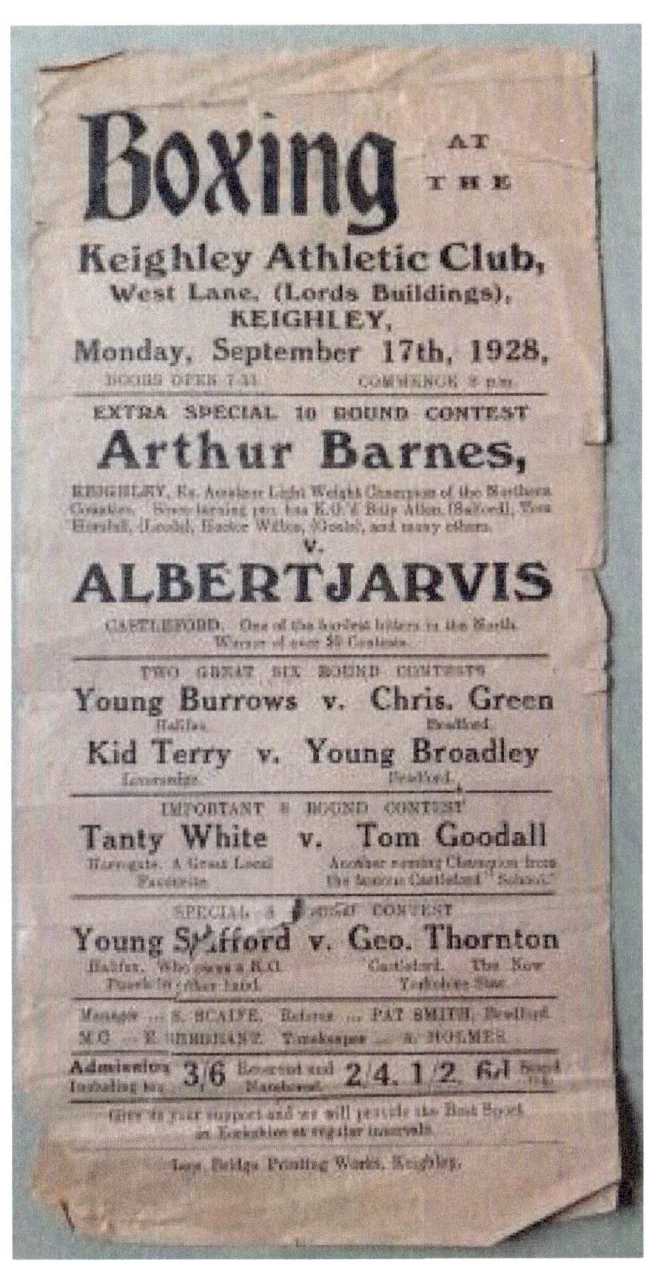

Freddie Irving (below)

A popular local fighter in the early 1930s

Hal Bairstow (below) Bairstow, a respected and successful middleweight in the late 1930s came from Morton. Here he is flanked by his manager Harold Beckett.

Harry Wood (above) Pictured in 1913, Harry was actually born in Prussia but moved to Keighley with his English father and brother, Herbert, when his mother died. The brothers were later tool fitters, but Harry was a well known Keighley boxer and had competed in 61 professional contests between 1913 and 1916. Sadly he was killed in action on 15th September 1916 while fighting for his adopted country.

Crosshills boxer **Gary Felvus** (left) had just been selected for the English senior boxing team to meet the United States at Gloucester when he was photographed for *The Keighley News* on 6th October 1981.

Keighley Boxing Club around 1977

Those in the photo include; *Mo, Alan Copperthwaite, John Daly, Gary Felvis, Lee Pickles, Andrew Reid. Michael Bland, Nigel Cutler, Chris Narey, David Binns, Stuart Gunning. Tommy Thompson, Lyndon Hedge, Sean Haughey, Tony Flaherty, Kevin Ryan, Joe Green, Jimmy Manley, Michael Stack, Peter Cutler, Richard Dudman, David Cottam* (Courtesy of Stephen Kennedy).

An advert for a boxing match between **Sapper George Clar** and **Harry Chester**, which took place at the town's Baths Hall in December 1920. The swimming pool was covered, and drained, when hosting boxing matches and regular dances.

CYCLING

Keighley Cycling Club

Keighley Cycling Club was founded in 1884. Club members (minus its lady members) are seen here outside their original wooden headquarters, both photographs taken early in the 1890s

Keighley Road Club Membership Card 1928

This particular card belonged to N Wells (Courtesy of Keighley Local History Society)

OFFICIALS, 1928.

President:
Mr. T. SHALLIS, Keighley.

Hon. Secretary and Treasurer:
Mr. C. H. RHODES, 7, Mornington Street, Keighley.

Committee:
Messrs. R. Howard, L. Sale, F. Butterfield,
A. R. Wilkinson, John Smith.

Hon Press Secretary: Mr. P. Heaton.

N.C.U. Delegates:
Messrs. C. H. Rhodes, R. Howard, F. Butterfield.

OBJECT.

The "KEIGHLEY ROAD CLUB" is a mixed club whose main object be to encourage Cycling in the Keighley and District.

RULES.

1.—That the name of this Club be the "KEIGHLEY ROAD CLUB."
2.—The age limit 14 years and upwards.
3.—That the Executive shall consist of a President, Secretary, and a Committee of Five members to be elected at the Annual General Meeting in each year.
4.—The Annual General Meeting be called the first week in each year.
5.—The Subscription be 4/- including N.C.U Affiliation Fee and Keighley Road Club Badge.
6.—Any candidate for membership must be proposed by a member and passed by the committee.
7.—The Subscription to be paid within one month from date of election.
8.—All Subscriptions become due on the first day of January, 1929.
9.—The runs to be selected monthly by the Committee, from suggestions handed in by the members, each suggestion to be written clearly on paper and signed by the suggesting party.
10.—The Runs will appear weekly in the 'Keighley News.'
11.—The Committee have power to expel any member whose behaviour is considered detrimental to the club.
12.—Any member who fails to renew his or her subscription is requested to return the badge and one shilling will be refunded.
13.—No Member is fully registered until he has received a National Cyclists Union Card.
14.—That the Executive shall have power to fill any vacancy that may occur during the year.
15.—Anything which may arise and not provided for in these rules shall be considered and decided upon by the executive.

All runs start from Albert Street.
Saturday afternoon runs, impromptu 2 p.m.

Puncture

A photograph taken in the early 1900s during a Keighley Cycling Club outing

Keighley Road Club in the 1950's & 60s

All of the images on the following five pages are courtesy of Margaret Barrett (nee Holden)

During the 1950s, club members would meet in a wooden hut at Parkwood on a Wednesday and enjoy a weekly 'picnic'.

Teenagers Bill & Margaret Holden on their first club run (right)

Bill Holden getting a push off

Fun and games on two wheels, three wheels (Eric Shackleton riding that one), and on a tandem…

Keighley Road Club days out

Top, *Helen Bairstow, Margaret Holden & Dora Redman.*

Middle: Taking a breather in the countryside.

Bottom: The whole club photographed at Malham on the occasion of the club Christmas dinner.

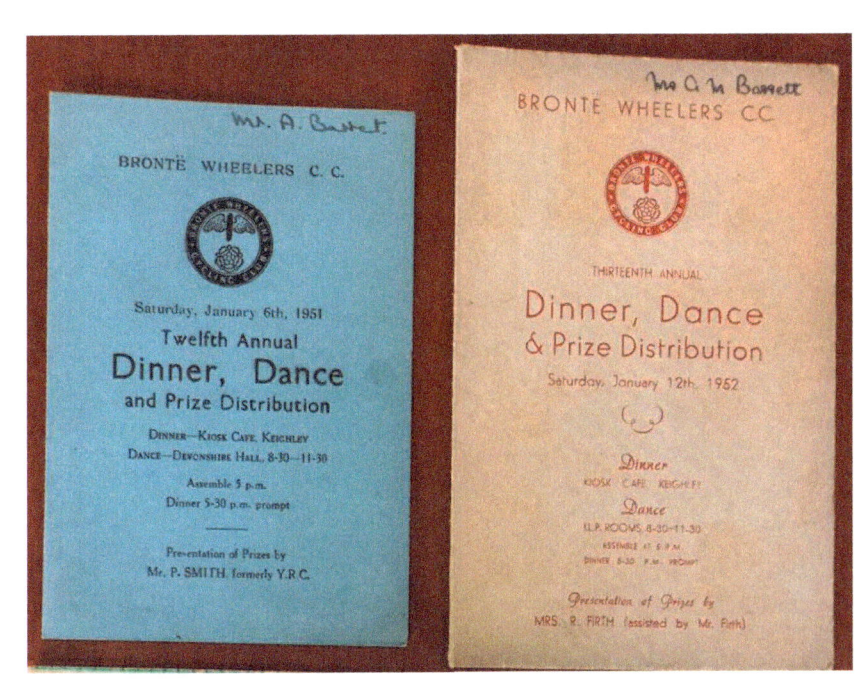

Left: Examples of cycling club Dinner, Dance & Prize Giving evenings.

Below: Keighley Road Club 25 Mile Time Trial handicap races

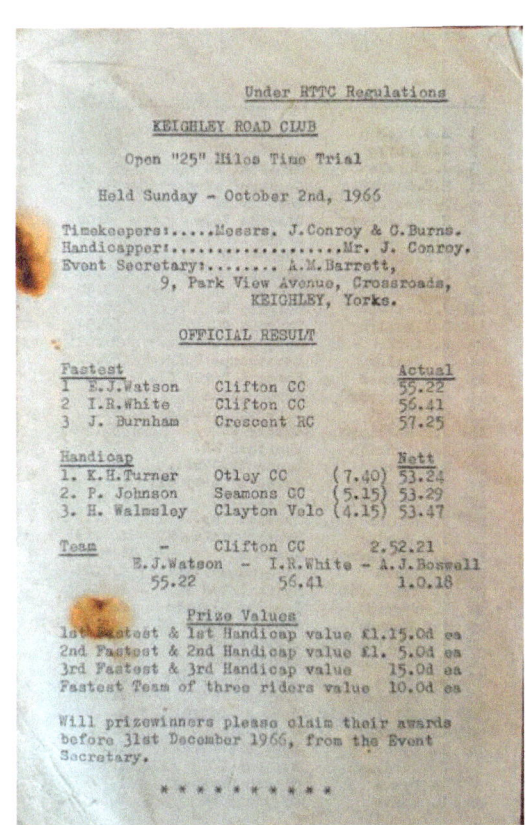

BRONTË WHEELERS C.C.

Saturday, January 6th, 1951

Twelfth Annual
Dinner, Dance
and Prize Distribution

DINNER—KIOSK CAFE, KEIGHLEY
DANCE—DEVONSHIRE HALL, 8-30—11-30

Assemble 5 p.m.
Dinner 5-30 p.m. prompt

Presentation of Prizes by
Mr. P. SMITH, formerly Y.R.C.

BRONTË WHEELERS CC

THIRTEENTH ANNUAL
Dinner, Dance
& Prize Distribution

Saturday, January 12th, 1952

Dinner
KIOSK CAFE, KEIGHLEY

Dance
E.L.P. ROOMS, 8-30—11-30
ASSEMBLE AT 5 P.M.
DINNER 5-30 P.M. PROMPT

Presentation of Prizes by
MRS. R. FIRTH (assisted by Mr. Firth)

Under RTTC Regulations

KEIGHLEY ROAD CLUB

Open "25" Miles Time Trial

Held Sunday – October 2nd, 1966

Timekeepers:....Messrs. J.Conroy & C.Burns.
Handicapper:..................Mr. J. Conroy.
Event Secretary:........ A.M.Barrett,
    9, Park View Avenue, Crossroads,
        KEIGHLEY, Yorks.

OFFICIAL RESULT

Fastest		Actual
1 E.J.Watson	Clifton CC	55.22
2 I.R.White	Clifton CC	56.41
3 J. Burnham	Crescent RC	57.25

Handicap			Nett
1. K.H.Turner	Otley CC	(7.40)	53.24
2. P. Johnson	Seamons CC	(5.15)	53.29
3. H. Walmsley	Clayton Velo	(4.15)	53.47

Team   Clifton CC   2.52.21
    E.J.Watson – I.R.White – A.J.Boswell
       55.22   56.41   1.0.18

Prize Values
1st Fastest & 1st Handicap value £1.15.0d ea
2nd Fastest & 2nd Handicap value £1. 5.0d ea
3rd Fastest & 3rd Handicap value   15.0d ea
Fastest Team of three riders value 10.0d ea

Will prizewinners please claim their awards before 31st December 1966, from the Event Secretary.

* * * * * * * * *

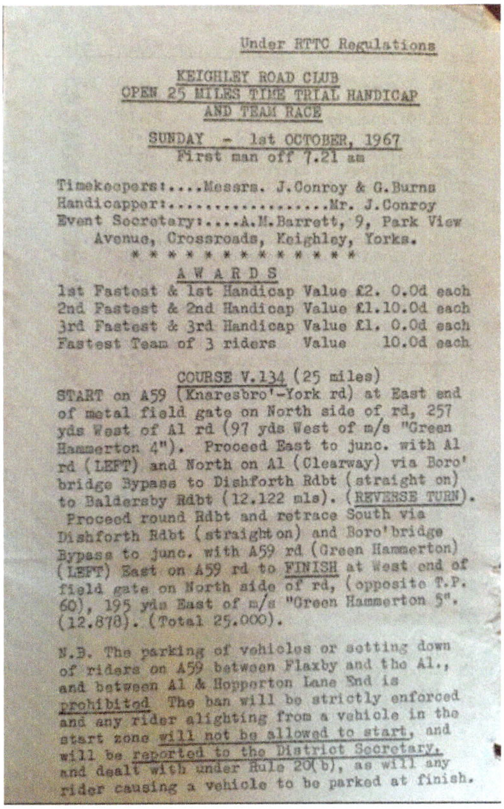

Under RTTC Regulations

KEIGHLEY ROAD CLUB
OPEN 25 MILES TIME TRIAL HANDICAP
AND TEAM RACE

SUNDAY – 1st OCTOBER, 1967
First man off 7.21 am

Timekeepers:....Messrs. J.Conroy & G.Burns
Handicapper:..................Mr. J.Conroy
Event Secretary:....A.M.Barrett, 9, Park View
    Avenue, Crossroads, Keighley, Yorks.
* * * * * * * * * *
AWARDS
1st Fastest & 1st Handicap Value £2. 0.0d each
2nd Fastest & 2nd Handicap Value £1.10.0d each
3rd Fastest & 3rd Handicap Value £1. 0.0d each
Fastest Team of 3 riders   Value   10.0d each

COURSE V.134 (25 miles)
START on A59 (Knaresbro'-York rd) at East end of metal field gate on North side of rd, 257 yds West of A1 rd (97 yds West of m/s "Green Hammerton 4"). Proceed East to junc. with A1 rd (LEFT) and North on A1 (Clearway) via Boro'bridge Bypass to Dishforth Rdbt (straight on) to Baldersby Rdbt (12.122 mls). (REVERSE TURN). Proceed round Rdbt and retrace South via Dishforth Rdbt (straight on) and Boro'bridge Bypass to junc. with A59 rd (Green Hammerton) (LEFT) East on A59 rd to FINISH at West end of field gate on North side of rd, (opposite T.P. 60), 195 yds East of m/s "Green Hammerton 5". (12.878). (Total 25.000).

N.B. The parking of vehicles or setting down of riders on A59 between Flaxby and the A1., and between A1 & Hopperton Lane End is prohibited. The ban will be strictly enforced and any rider alighting from a vehicle in the start zone will not be allowed to start, and will be reported to the District Secretary, and dealt with under Rule 20(b), as will any rider causing a vehicle to be parked at finish.

Left: Alan Barrett is seen en route to winning Keighley Inter Club roller cycling competition. Here he is held by Bill Fielding.

Below: Keighley Road Club's Annual Dinner brochure, 1967.

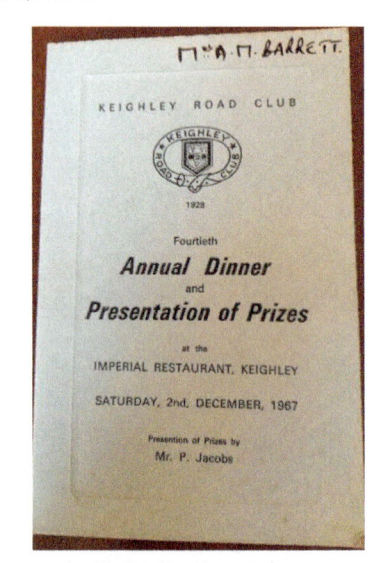

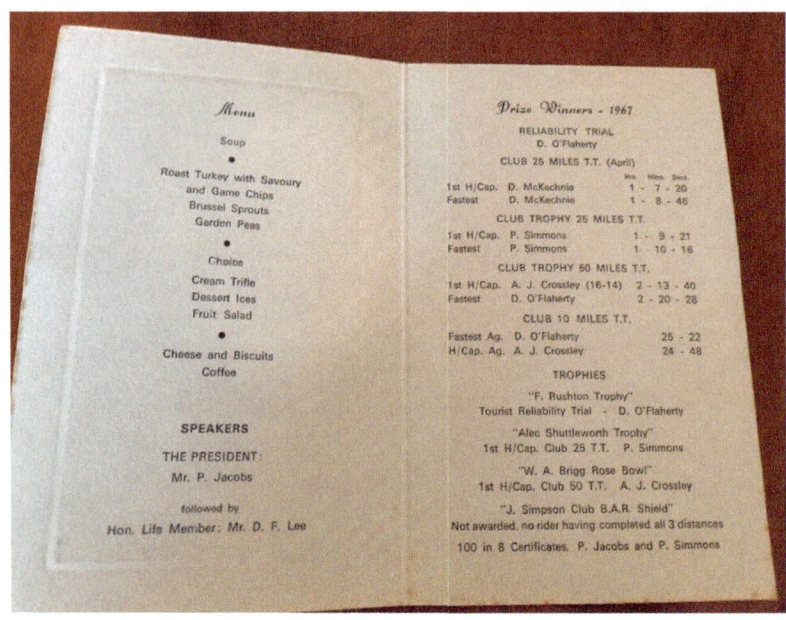

Keighley Velo

An early photo of the Keighley Velo club, featuring their original jerseys. These were actually recycled rugby shirts, with the Keighley Velo logo sowed on by Doug Petty's mother. Doug is second from right.

Keighley Velo club outing

This photograph was taken at The Marquis of Granby, at Riddlesden

(Both photos on this page courtesy of Liz Spencer Petty)

Croad Automatic Trophy

Muriel Fretwell, wife of Peter Fretwell, the proprietor of International Cycle Sport, presents the Croad Automatic Trophy (for the winner of the Keighley & District Cycling Association Championship) to **Pete Jepson** (Keighley Velo), who shared the trophy with **Tom McDonald** (St Christopher's). McDonald is on the left, looking at the camera, and he is the father of successful local runner Stuart McDonald. The exact year is unknown (Courtesy of Liz Spencer Petty).

Dave Tate (left), **Tom Farrar** (Leeds, centre) & **Doug Petty** (right).

Edward Ackroyd

Edward Ackroyd was a member of the Bronte Wheelers cycling club. This photo was taken in Easingwold, the day that the UK went to War (3rd September 1939). *'He told us that people were shouting out to tell him'*, says Wendy Halloway, Edward's daughter, who provided the photograph.

Keighley Road Club, 1959

The photo includes *Margaret Barrett, Harry McKechnie, Ian McKechnie, Peter Simmons, Alan Smith, Geoff Burns, Alan Simons, Gordon Brooks, Gordon 'Gid' Sheffield, Mervyn Coates, Alan Barrett, Eddie 'Kronk' Atkinson, Alec Crossley, Peter Williams, Derek Bown, John Brooks, Jack 'Nuff' Simpson, Colin Hesketh, Eric 'Shack' Shackleton* (Courtesy of Derek Bown).

Keighley was certainly a hotbed of cycling from the 1950s. Left and at the bottom are images from the programme for a popular local road race, while The first Keighley Festival of Cycling Weekend was held at Victoria Park on 7th & 8th October 1967.

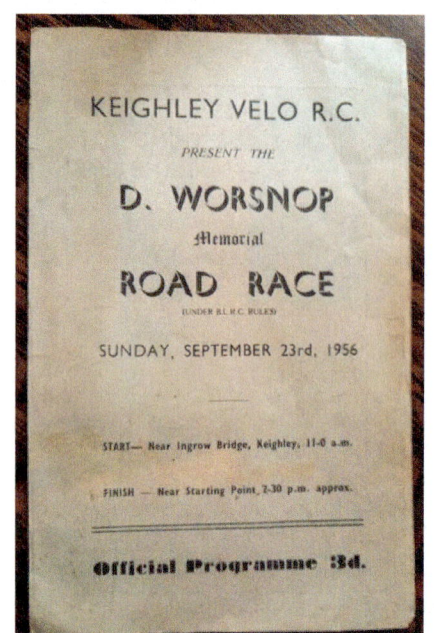

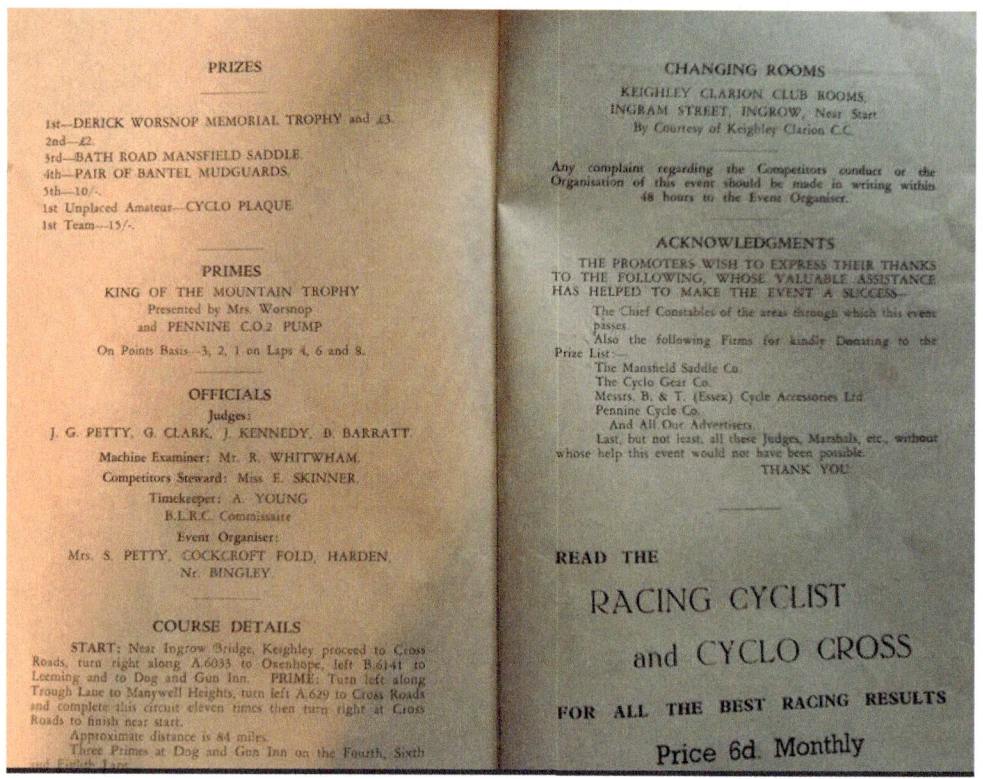

October 4th & 5th 1969
Keighley Festival of Cycling Weekend

The third annual Keighley Festival of Cycling Weekend was organised by the Keighley & Craven Cycling Association. It included criterium racing, cyclo-cross and the notorious Thwaites Brow hill climb. Riders came from all around the UK to compete.

From the programme for Saturday: *'At 5.00 pm, the second annual Thwaites Brow Hill Climb will be promoted by Keighley Velo R. C. (under R. T. T. C. rules) on the dreaded, cobbled, Thwaites 'wall'. The start is at Thwaites, Worth Village, Keighley (1/2 mile from Victoria Park) and the finish is at Moss Carr, Long Lee, Keighley. Come along and see these boys defying gravity!!'*

Amateur riders from Keighley included C Grayson, Dave Tate, J Cuthbert, D. Horsman, A Knowles, G Fox and J Wray from Keighley Velo, and P Kennedy, J. Holmes, G Halls, Tom McDonald and P Loftus from Keighley St. Christopher's.

Below: Cyclists at the start in the main event (Courtesy of Liz Spencer Petty).

KEIGHLEY & CRAVEN CYCLING ASSOCIATION.

ANNUAL 50 MILE TIME TRIAL.

Sunday July 12th 1970 at 6.30 a.m.
Under R.T.T.C. regulations.

Timekeeper:-	D.Bown Esq.	Marshals:- Members and
Handicapper:-	J.B.Cuthbert Esq.	friends of the
Event Sec:-	J.B.Cuthbert Esq,	Association.
	19, Heath Grove,	
	East Morton,	
	Keighley, Yorks.	
	B.D.20 5.T.A.	

Course V.956:- Start opposite lamp standard, 70 yards S.E. of Steeton Traffic Lights on A.629. On A.629 to Alice Street, Keighley. Turn round manhole cover and retrace to junction of A.629 & A.6068. Left on A.6068 to junction with Station Road. Right on Station Road to rejoin A.629. Left on A.629 to junction with A.59. Left on A.59 to junction with A.56. Left on A.56 to turn in road 65 yards W. of junction with unclassified road signposted Elslack. Retrace on A.56 and A.59 to rejoin A.629. Left on A.629 to junction with A.65. Left on A.65 to turn in road opposite mark 'TTT' approx 1½ miles N.W. of Maypole Hotel, Long Preston. Retrace on A.65 and A.629 to finish on A.629 at lane end 50 yards S.E. of White House Farm, Kildwick.

No.	Name	Club	H/cap All.	Time Off.
1.	C.K.Clegg.	Keighley St CCCC.	30.00.	6.31.
2.	R.Crane.	Keighley St CCCC.	21.40.	.32.
3.	A.Rostron.	Skipton C.C.	6.40.	.33.
4.	P.Kennedy.	Keighley St CCCC.	10.50.	.34.
5.	D.Mitchell.	Keighley Velo R.C.	9.10.	.35.
6.	J.Holmes.	Keighley St CCCC.	10.50.	.36.
7.	B.Northing.	Keighley Velo R.C.	2.05.	.37.
8.	H.Durkin.	Keighley St CCCC.	10.00.	.38.
9.	J.Wray.	Keighley Velo R.C.	2.30.	.39.
10.	J.D.Smith.	Keighley St CCCC.	5.25.3.45	6.40.
11.	T.A.Cutler.	Skipton C.C.	4.10.	.41.
12.	J.B.Cuthbert.	Keighley St CCCC.	5.00.7.30	.42.
13.	T.Sneath.	Craven Clarion.	Scr.	.43.

Frame numbers will be worn. Please allow time for fitting.

Please park cars at the FINISH and ride to the start.

Your attention is drawn to R.T.T.C. regulation 47... Company and paced riding.

Please take care on the roundabout at the bottom of High Street in Skipton. This is very slippery even in dry conditions.

Any complaints about this event must be made, IN WRITING, to the event secretary within 48 hours.

(Courtesy of Derek Bown)

Derek Bown, competing in York on behalf of Keighley Road Club in 1959 (Courtesy of Derek Bown).

Keighley 'Road' Club outing 1950s

(Both photos courtesy of Derek Bown)

Lewis Whitaker & other local cyclists, taken in the 1940s and 50s

(Photos courtesy of Margaret and Melissa Whitaker /Keighley Local History Society)

Right: Lewis Whitaker competes in a cycling race, believed to be along West Lane, Keighley. 1950s.

Right: Lewis Whitaker about to set off in a cycling race along Skipton Road. Circa 1955. Frank Kennedy is holding Lewis before the push off and Ronnie Sherlock is standing to the right with the stopwatch. The Essoldo Cinema (now Picture House cinema), the Keighley News building, and the clock tower of the Mechanics' Institute can be seen in the background.

Below: Keighley cyclists lined up outside Shuttleworth's cycle shop on Skipton Road, Keighley. 1950s. *From left to right: John Boland, Frank Kennedy, Kenny Roberts, n/k, n/k, Jack Kennedy, Lewis Whitaker, Paul Kennedy, n/k.* The Kennedy brothers (Frank, Jack, and Paul), were among the founders of the St Christopher's Cycling Club in 1946

Fred Norton & Keighley Road Club, late 1950s

(Photos courtesy of Thelma Norton Spencer)

Freddie Norton leads the way ahead, and in the pack, below left

Below: Somewhere in the Dales, this photograph of Freddie illustrates better than anything how leisurewear has changed over the years.

Keighley Road Club presentation evening, late 1950s

From left to right, Fred Norton, Alan Barrett, John Brookes, Alec Crossley, Peter Williams, Peter Jacobs, Colin Hesketh.

Keighley Velo team around 1967

G Fox, D Horsman, M Maude, R Crave

Keighley RC-ICS Magazine

From left, Simon Thomas, Paul Milnes, Des Fretwell and Steve Thomas.

Keighley St Christopher's CC

Photographed are the Kennedy brothers Paul, Frank, Patrick & Jack. Their father was the founder of the Keighley section of the St Christopher's club (this and the photo below courtesy of Veronica Kennedy)

Left: Frank Kennedy in action

201

Races passing through the district

(All 6 of these are courtesy of Terry Hanson)

Leeds Classic 1995

The peloton conquers Cock Hill.

Kelloggs Tour of Britain 1998

The riders are seen above Oxenhope

Tony the tiger heading the Cavalcade

202

Brontë Cycle Race 1990

The riders are seen climbing out of Leeming.

Wincanton Classic Cycle Race August 1992

View from the top of the Crag near Crossroads.

Tour of Britain 2004

Again, riders are seen on top of Cock Hill.

Tour de France 2014

The second stage of the 101st Tour de France, came through Keighley on Sunday 6th July, 2014. The route then made it way up Halifax Road to Cross Roads, through Haworth towards Stanbury, up across Penistone Hill, down to Oxenhope before the climb up to *Cote de Cock Hill* before descending to Hebden Bridge. The image below shows crowds at Hardings Road roundabout as the peloton passes through.

The two images opposite show the riders as they travelled along Skipton Road (both courtesy of Jenny Beaumont)

204

The Tour de France photographs on the following two pages were all taken by Terry Hanson.

La Caravane at the bottom of Cock Hill, Oxenhope

La Caravane climbing Cock Hill

Spectators waiting at *Cote de Cock Hill*

Spectators – and the local constabulary - waiting at *Cote de Cock Hill*

The Peloton begins the descent of Cock Hill

Emblem near Damems, taken from Hainworth

Tour de Yorkshire

In 2015 the Tour de Yorkshire came through Oxenhope, Haworth, Oakworth, Goose Eye, Sutton-in-Craven and Glusburn on the Stage Three route from Wakefield to Leeds; in 2017, Stage Three passed through Silsden, Riddlesden, Keighley, Cross Roads with Lees, Haworth, Marsh, Oxenhope, and Leeming on the route from Bradford to Wakefield. The 2018 event saw the Stage Four pass through Oxenhope, Haworth, Oakworth, Sutton-in-Craven and Crosshills on the route from Halifax to Leeds; and in 2019, Stage Four came through Leeming, Oxenhope, Haworth, Oakworth, Holme House, Laycock and Sutton-in-Craven on the route from Halifax to Leeds. Photo shows riders ascending Haworth main Street in 2018.

Both photographs on this page are courtesy of Jenny Beaumont. They show the cyclists leaving the Victoria Park roundabout in the 2017 event.

OTHER SPORTS

Knurr & Spell, Keighley Tarn 1968

The Keighley district was a hotbed of Knurr & Spell, a sport that can be traced back to the 14th century. Its popularity surged in the 18th and 19th centuries, especially in Yorkshire. Here we see a demonstration event, held in much later times.

In Knurr and Spell, the 'spell' is a levered wooden trap which launches a small, hard ball known as the 'knurr.' Players used a long bat, traditionally made of ash or lancewood, to hit the knurr as far as possible. Timing and precision are of the essence, as players must strike the airborne knurr at the right moment.

Prince Smith & Stell's Bowling Club

Photographed at Strong Close around 1934 (Courtesy of Keighley & District Local History Society).

Lund Park Bowlers 1945

(Courtesy of Brian Moate)

Lund Park Bowlers 1950

Names include *Arthur Clayton, Binns Bancroft, Fred Robinson, Edgar Storton* (Courtesy of Brian Moate).

Lund Park Ladies Bowls 1950

Names include *Mrs Gee, Mrs Rothera, Mrs Varley, Mrs Robinson, Mrs Eunice Hutchinson, Mrs Ratcliffe, Mrs Longden, Mrs Hutchinson, Mrs Hargreaves, Julie Clayton* (Courtesy of Brian Moate, whose mother Sally is front right).

Whinswood Bowling Club 2002

Winners of the Ken Johnson Cup. Left to right: *Keith Humphrey, Derek Burgess, Arthur Brown, Margaret Slater, John Smith (Captain), Jenny Taylor, Keith Ridding, Sue Finnie, Geoff Smith, Ted Barnes, Graham Whitaker, Bob Scott.*

The photograph was part of the Vine Tavern Collection

Silsden Bowling Green

Postcard by R Dewhirst, from between the wars

LUND PARK BOWLING CLUB   SEPTEMBER 2015

David Myers, Gordon Lloyd, Peter Sands, Olive Lansdall, Alan Robinson, Steve Lloyd, Jack Duncan, Bill Duckworth, Harry Goldsborough, Derek Bown

Hazel Myers, Steve Broadley, Maureen Bailey, Brian Dobson, Margaret Dobson, Stuart Hall, Leslie Dowthwaite, Jack Whitehead, Martin Cleasby

Terry Senior, Christine Johnson, Bob Moate, Malcolm Walsh, Eileen Whiteoak, Alan King, Hazel Cartwright, Carol Harrison, Melvyn Johnson, Derek Burgess

Greenhead Grammar School Under 19 Volleyball team,

Photographed for *The Keighley News* in February 1982, the team had recently won the Yorkshire Schools title. The sport was encouraged within the school by the newly arrived woodwork teacher Dave Speers, himself an English International. Left to right: *Philip Wood, Matthew Sharp, Andrew Parnham, Dave Speers, Richard Malin, Stephen Ives, Mark Mothersdale.*

Brian Graham

A 7th Dan, Shorinji Kempo, Jiu Jitsu, Brian Graham brought the sport to Keighley in 1969 and taught children and adults up until 2005, the year he sadly passed away. He also had Jiu Jitsu clubs in Universities all over the country, as well as a number in Canada (Courtesy of Michelle Hughes)

Ingrow St John's Table Tennis 1979

(Courtesy of David Martin)

Keith Martin, a well known face in local table tennis circles, winning the Keighley championship and later taking on the role of President of the Keighley Table Tennis League from the 1960s through to the 1980s (Courtesy of David Martin).

League President Keith Martin presents prizes in the 1982 Keighley & District Table Tennis Championship, held in April of that year. *From left to right: Keith Martin, Simon Rix (Riddlesden), Steve Taylor, Roy Warrener, and Andrew Brook (Long Lee)* (Courtesy of David Martin).

Worth Valley Table Tennis team 1983. *Keith Martin, D Frogbrook, E Klava* (Courtesy of David Martin).

Keighley Girls' Grammar School Netball Team 1947/48

(Courtesy of Keighley Local History Society)

Sarah Longbottom

Girl Guide Sarah Longbottom (now Sarah Thomas) following the presentation of a plate inscribed: *'Presented to Sarah Longbottom, 1st Riddlesden Guides, Winner of the National Tennis Tournament 1981, from West Yorkshire North'*. Sarah went on to represent Yorkshire for some 15 years, represented Great Britain as a junior on three occasions and also played for England (Courtesy of Keighley Local History Society).

Simon Ickringill started playing at Keighley Tennis Club at the age of nine, before moving to Ilkley LTC in 1974. He played for the club's men's first team from age 19 and became head coach in 1981, a position he held for over 40 years until his retirement in 1993. He first played for Yorkshire in 1979, and was Yorkshire Men's Singles Champion no fewer than eight times. He represented England in Home Nations events and Great Britain at in veterans age groups. At the age of 49 he won the National over 45s title. (Courtesy of Ilkley Lawn Tennis & Squash Club www.iltsc.co.uk)

Riddlesden Tennis Club 1981

This photograph was taken on 27th September 1981, during the club's finals day. They are (L to R) *Matt Barnard, Gerry Bawcombe, Nicola Brook, Beryl Bawcombe and Ian Wilson* (Courtesy of Keighley Local History Society).

Riddlesden Tennis Club around 1983
(Courtesy of Darren Whitaker)

Veronica Kennedy, World Champion

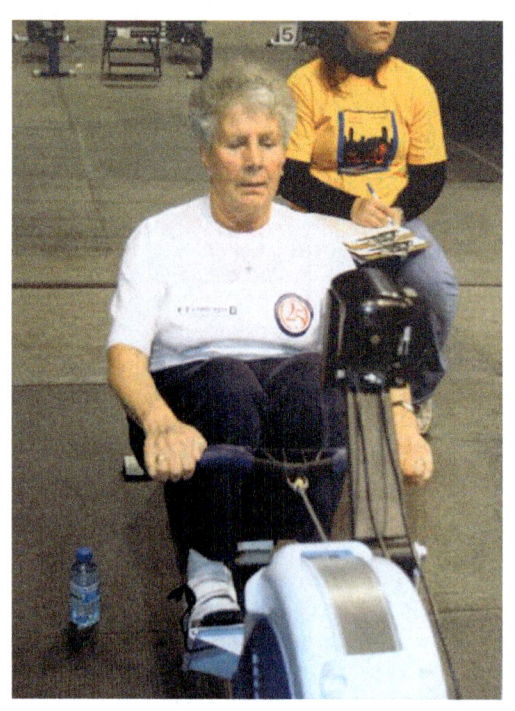

In 2006 Veronica Kennedy, at the time aged 71, won the World Indoor Rowing championship for her age group in Boston, USA. Over 2,000 rowers took part in the event, including her son, boxer Stephen Kennedy (who is also pictured below). She had only taken up the sport the previous year and had suffered a stroke three years earlier (All three photos are courtesy of Veronica herself).

Trials Biking

Oxenhope trials biker Eric Robshaw is seen here in action, and with just some of his silverware, which he won with the Bradford vagabonds club.

Below, motor-cyclist Sam Clayton, towing his sleigh rider, Robshaw himself, attempts to overtake his opponent at Haworth Round Table Gala in the early 1960s. It is hard to imagine this being allowed in this day and age.

All three photographs on this page are courtesy of Eric Robshaw.

Gymnastic clubs became popular in the early 1900s. The **Lees & Cross Roads Institute Gymnastic team**, had it survived to this day, would be in a spot of bother if they tried to repeat this exercise in the middle of the main road through the village.

Highfield School Badminton team 1962

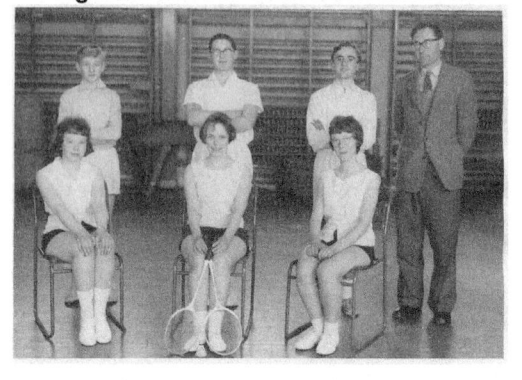

Below, **Keighley Golf Club**, featured on a postcard, around 1920

The spread on following page is from *The Bradford Bystander*, 1965, showing players at Keighley Golf Club. The players photographed are A R Illingworth (Club President), John Sunderland, J Emmott (Yorkshire County Player), Norman Sunderland, Frank Anderton, J McDougall, Ken Waterhouse (Club Captain), Harry Anderton (Rabbits Captain), John Price, Dennis Roper, S Dennison, J A Greenwood, H P Clough, Allan Denby, Denis Taylor, S Blythe, Dr J R Fountain, J Goodall, R Mitchell (Yorkshire County Player), Philip Vaux, Jack Green, Mrs J A Greenwood, Mrs J I Dewhirst, W Lord, Norman Lumb and E T McCartney. The *Bradford Bystander* began publishing in 1964 and continued at least into the 1970s (Courtesy of the Keighley and District Local History Society digital archive).

KEIGHLEY
GOLF
CLUB

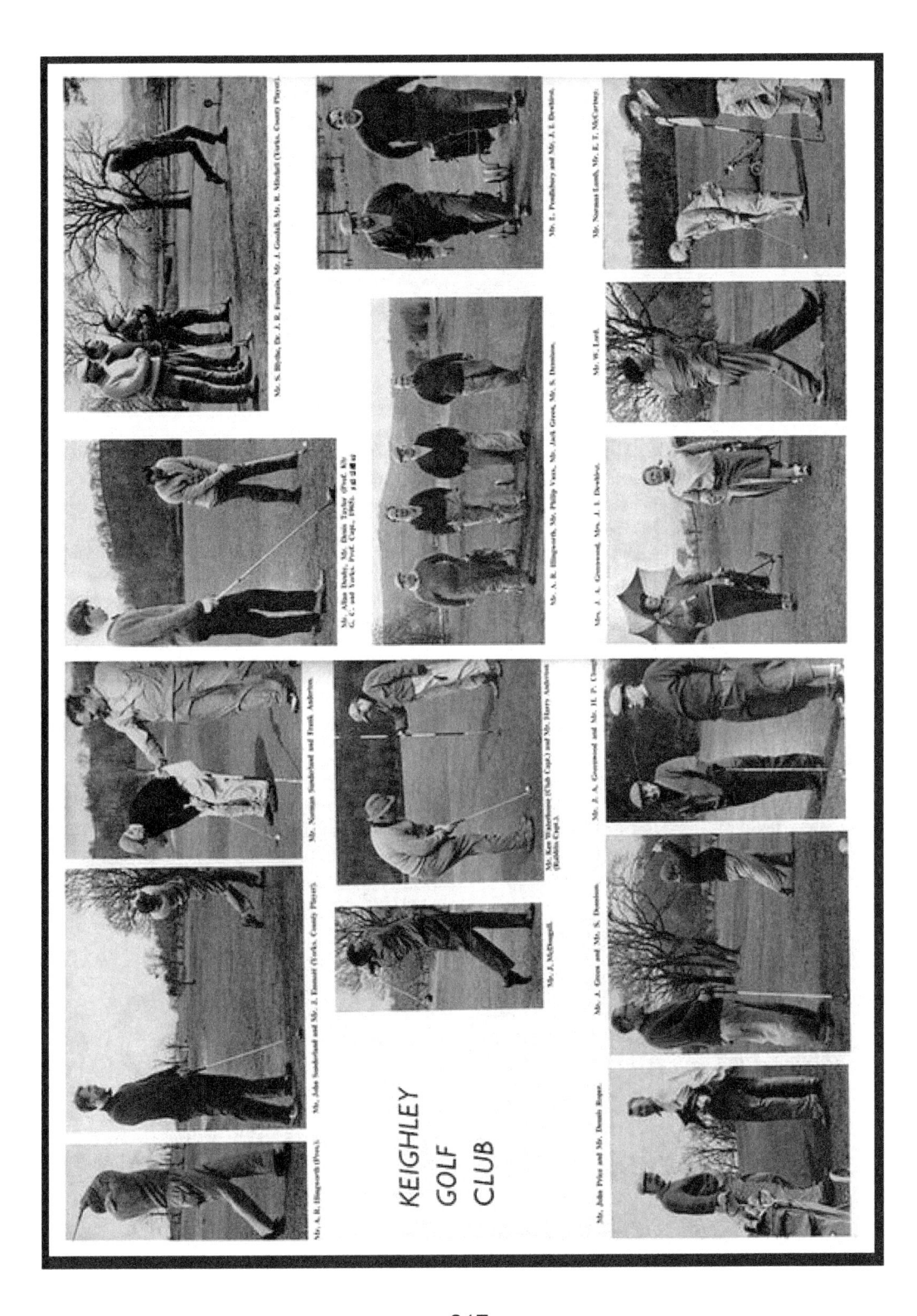

Swire Smith Middle School Under 13s Badminton team 1982

From left to right: Neil Kennedy, Angela Winterburn, Andrew Blowes, Charlotte Broadhead, Janet Heaton, and Sharron Jessup

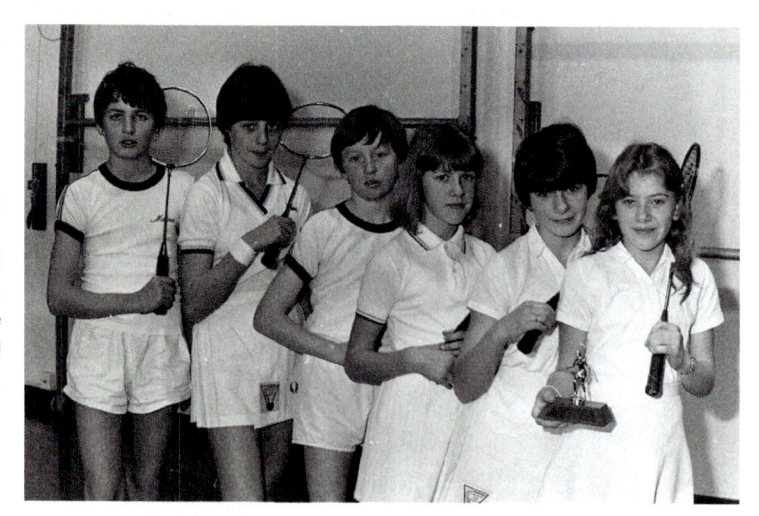

Left: **Michelle Bhowmick**, who became the Yorkshire Under 13's badminton champion early in 1982, seen here with the John Foster Shield. She represented Yorkshire in a competition in Belgium in Easter that year.

Right: **Amanda Thompson** & **Joanne Pickering** of Grange Middle School with certificates and a trophy from the Bradford Schools Gymnastic Association Under 12s competition in February 1983.

Left: **Grange Middle School Synchronised Swimming Team** around 1983. From left to right: *Cheryl Pickering, Katie Wishart & Corinne Hey.* Katie herself went on to gain international honours in the sport, and was part of the British team that finished fourth in the Women Team Artistic Swimming European Championship in August 1995 in Wien, Austria (Courtesy of Katie herself)

Keighley Angling Club Annual Supper Card, 1898.

The late Laurence Brocklesby, who was President of Keighley Angling Club and Keighley and District Local History Society researched the history of the Angling Club. He wrote, *'We have evidence that there were two clubs which amalgamated in 1883, previously called the Silsden and the Eastburn Angling Clubs. On the first day of December 1868, an indenture was signed by the Riparian owners and occupiers of fishing rights on the River Aire and the River Worth granting a lease of fishing to the Keighley Angling Club. These waters stretched from Bingley right up the valley. Two of the owners being, in 1883, Lord Hothfield of Skipton Castle and the Duke of Devonshire from Bolton Abbey.*

Matches were held once a year, mainly for trout. These were weighed in at the Roebuck Hotel in Utley. The weights used on the scales were lead shot and these were used until proper scales were purchased. One thing which happened each year was the presentation of a plate of trout to each land owner. In years when it was not possible to catch these, they were bought from a local fishmonger.'

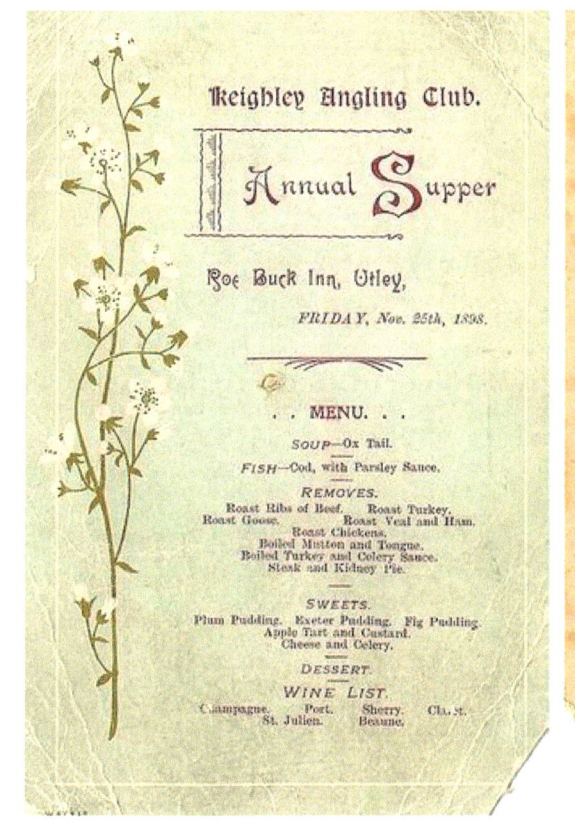

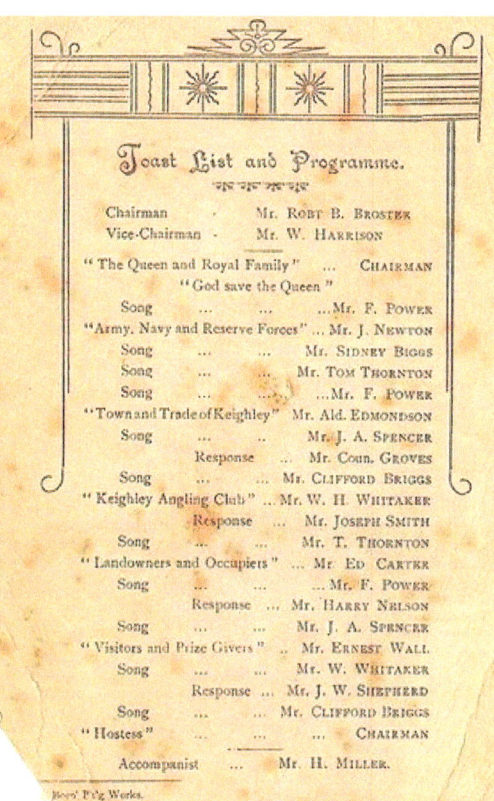

Keighley Angling Club.
Annual Supper

Roe Buck Inn, Utley,

FRIDAY, Nov. 25th, 1898.

. . MENU . .

SOUP—Ox Tail.

FISH—Cod, with Parsley Sauce.

REMOVES.
Roast Ribs of Beef.   Roast Turkey.
Roast Goose.   Roast Veal and Ham.
Roast Chickens.
Boiled Mutton and Tongue.
Boiled Turkey and Celery Sauce.
Steak and Kidney Pie.

SWEETS.
Plum Pudding.   Exeter Pudding.   Fig Pudding.
Apple Tart and Custard.
Cheese and Celery.

DESSERT.

WINE LIST.
Champagne.   Port.   Sherry.   Claret.
St. Julien.   Beaune.

Toast List and Programme.

Chairman	Mr. ROBT B. BROSTER
Vice-Chairman	Mr. W. HARRISON
"The Queen and Royal Family"	CHAIRMAN
"God save the Queen"	
Song	Mr. F. POWER
"Army, Navy and Reserve Forces"	Mr. J. NEWTON
Song	Mr. SIDNEY BIGGS
Song	Mr. TOM THORNTON
Song	Mr. F. POWER
"Town and Trade of Keighley"	Mr. Ald. EDMONDSON
Song	Mr. J. A. SPENCER
Response	Mr. Coun. GROVES
Song	Mr. CLIFFORD BRIGGS
"Keighley Angling Club"	Mr. W. H. WHITAKER
Response	Mr. JOSEPH SMITH
Song	Mr. T. THORNTON
"Landowners and Occupiers"	Mr. ED CARTER
Song	Mr. F. POWER
Response	Mr. HARRY NELSON
Song	Mr. J. A. SPENCER
"Visitors and Prize Givers"	Mr. ERNEST WALL
Song	Mr. W. WHITAKER
Response	Mr. J. W. SHEPHERD
Song	Mr. CLIFFORD BRIGGS
"Hostess"	CHAIRMAN
Accompanist	Mr. H. MILLER

Bocking Working Men's Club Angling Club 1981

The club was winner of the Northern Angling Cup, the trophy here being presented by branch president Arthur Gilman in September of that year. Club members include Frank Feather, Raymond Large, Mick Skinner, Royce Foster, Keith Ridding and Keith Abson (Courtesy of Keighley Local History Society digital archive).

Keighley Girls' Grammar School Tennis team 1948

(This and the photos on the following page are courtesy of Keighley Local History Society digital archive)

Keighley Girls' Grammar School Hockey 1943

Hockey Tournament in aid of the Red Cross. Sat 10th April 1943

Keighley Girls' Grammar School Hockey team 1970s

Keighley Girls' Grammar School Netball team 1970s

221

Keighley Boys' Grammar School Sports

All photographs here are courtesy of Helen Anstis. They all feature either her dad John Frankland, or his older brother Thomas. *'Tom , born 1912 , excelled at sports. He went on to be high up in the post office in Scotland. John, born 1921, wasn't a sportsman - though he did make the 2nd X1 rugby team. Pot holing was his thing later in life.'*, she says.

1st XV Rugby 1927/28

Back: Mr E Marsden, T Frankland, E V Cave, E Antrum, J E N Hooper, K J Hird, E Wade, Mr H E Hoyle. Middle: W A S Knowles, E Dawson, T K Smith (Captain), Mr T P Watson, W E Newsome (Vice Captain), E P Bramfit. Front: B Weatherhead, F Harrison, A C Robinson, A R Cave.

1st XV Rugby 1928/29

The team won 11 of its 19 matches that season (including a school record 86-0 win along the way). *Back: Mr H E Hoyle, G A Watson, N Balty, G E W Hird, N C Roberts, C G Frost, N Hughes, J E N Hooper, Mr E Marsden. Middle: T Frankland, E Antrum, T K Smith (Captain), Mr T P Watson, E P Bramfit (Vice Captain), E Dawson. Front: J H Smith, J C Coates, K Holmes, J Holmes, A R Cave.*

Cricket Team 1930

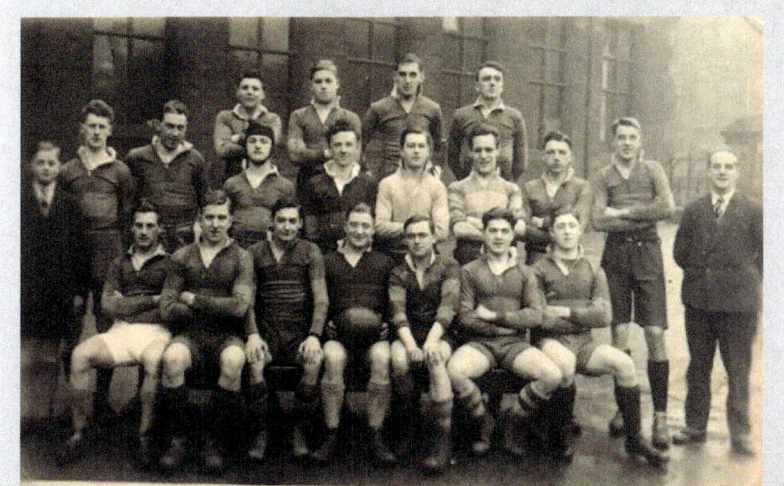

Rugby XV

Thomas Frankland is immediately behind the lad with the ball.

2ⁿᵈ XV Rugby 1939/40

John Frankland is front left, seated on the ground.

KBGS Athletics, 3rd June 1930

Thomas Frankland is in the middle in the hurdles race, and also seen in the high jump below in the school athletics day held at Keighley Cricket Club. In the background of the hurdles race can be seen the rugby posts at the former Threaproyd sports ground.

Keighley Swimming baths (the old ones)

Keighley Swimming Baths prior to demolition. These photographs were taken by Geoffrey Kitchen in 1990, the baths being closed in 1989 and demolished in 1995. The entrance here was located at the junction of Spencer Street with Highfield Street, although it had originally been on Albert Street until 1960, when the building was enlarged and remodelled. The site now contains houses known as Kendal Mellor Court.

The First class swimming pool was obviously the main pool, located just beyond the entrance. In winter it was covered and converted into a ballroom. The Second class swimming pool was located down the stairs beyond the entrance and was used a teaching pool for schoolchildren.

Kendal Mellor himself (photographed below) was a long-distance outdoor swimmer of some repute. Among his feats was a 16 hour 53 minute crossing of the English Channel from France to England in 1963. He was the first person to swim 37 km across the Canal de Menorca (Menorca Channel) that stretches between the Balearic islands of Menorca and Mallorca in the Mediterranean Sea in October 1968. He also participated in the ice swims held on the first Sunday after the New Year during the 1960s in Lea Dam, Lumbutts, near Hebden Bridge.

Bibliography

Ronnie Wharton, *Boxing In Leeds & Bradford*, 2001

Maurice Tillotson website https://tillotson.co.nz/

Tramlines, Yorkshire Tennis Newsletter, November 2023,

Keighley News, various editions

Elizabeth Gaskill, *The Life of Charlotte Bronte*, 1857

John Goulstone, *Football's Secret History*, 2001

Robert Holmes, *Keighley Past & Present*, 1858

Other Books by Rob Grillo

www.robgrillo.co.uk

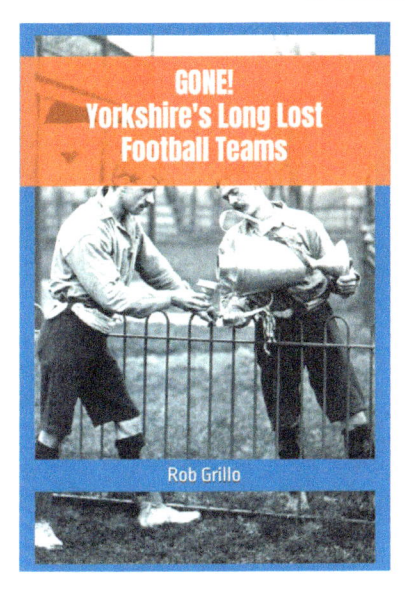

GONE – YORKSHIRE'S LONG LOST FOOTBALL TEAMS hardback & paperback

WEST YORKSHIRE'S LONG LOST RUGBY CLUBS hardback & paperback

CRUSTY FARMERS WITH PITCHFORKS hardback & paperback

A NOBLE WINTER'S GAME paperback

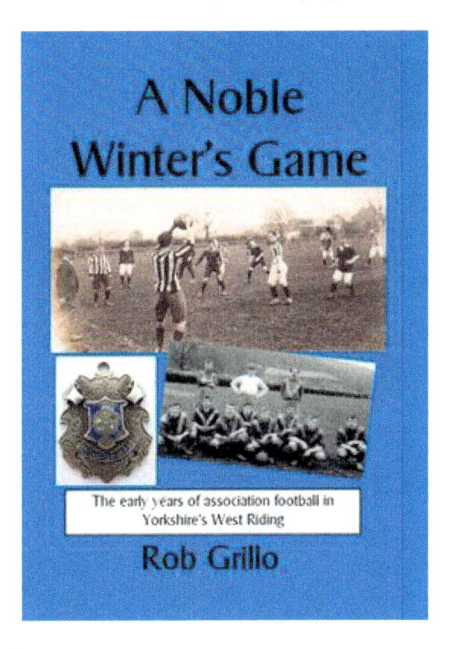

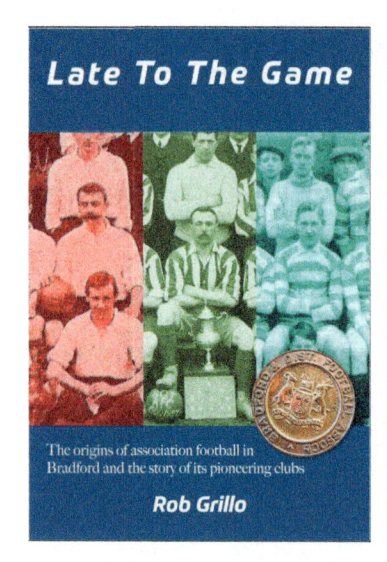

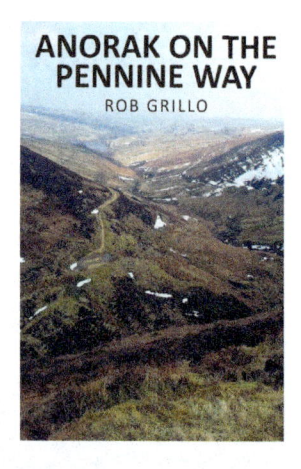

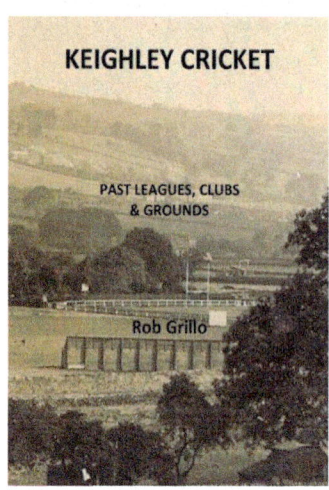

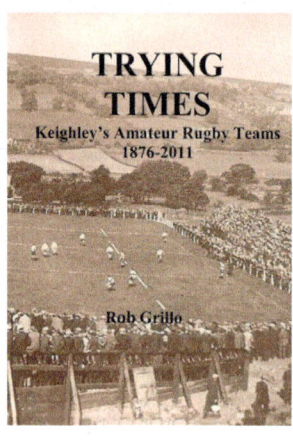

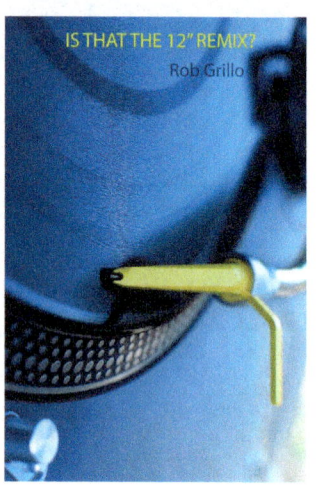

Out of Print

ANORAKNOPHOBIA

KEIGHLEY'S SOCCER HISTORY

CHASING GLORY – Keighley Soccer volume 1

GLORY DENIED - Keighley Soccer volume 2

STAYING THE DISTANCE – Distance Running in Keighley

100 YEARS ON

IS THAT THE 12" MIX

www.keighleyhistory.org.uk

The Society was formed in 2004 following the Centenary of Keighley Carnegie Library.

It was felt that a dedicated local history society would benefit Keighley and help to preserve and strengthen our vast and varied Heritage in Keighley and the Local Area.

The Society is a fully Constituted organisation, run by it's Committee on behalf of it's Members.

We aim to collect, preserve, understand and ultimately share the unique and interesting history of our local area. In the process we hope that people can learn how the areas relate to each other and how the ethos of the area has developed.

We hold monthly Speakers meetings on a variety of subjects relating to local history. These are open to everyone.

While we concentrate mainly on the Districts covered by the pre 1974 Keighley Borough Council, the history sometimes spreads to include other areas that have at times been linked to or administered from Keighley.

Over time members of the public have donated or let us copy their items and we have now have a large amount of material. This is stored at the Civic Centre and forms the Society's Archive

Our Physical Archives contain books, publications, documents, photographs, other media projects completed by members, and small objects relating to the area.

Over the years we have also amassed a Digital Archive, which provides for online research,

We also work with a number of local partners to help them open up their own Archives

230

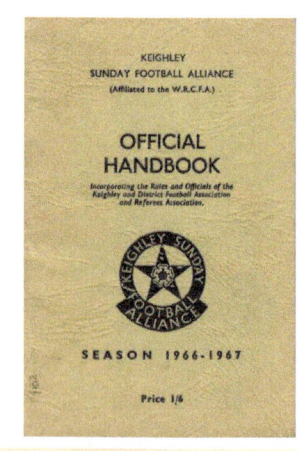

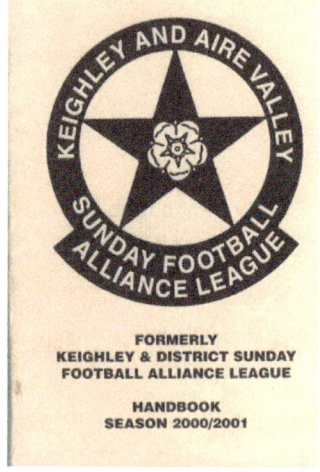

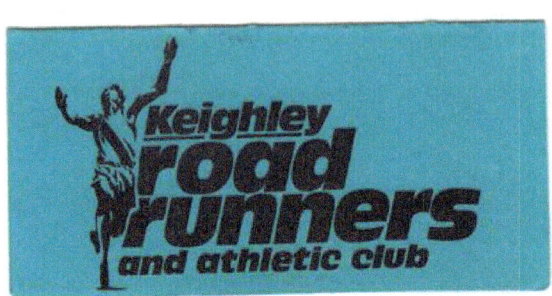

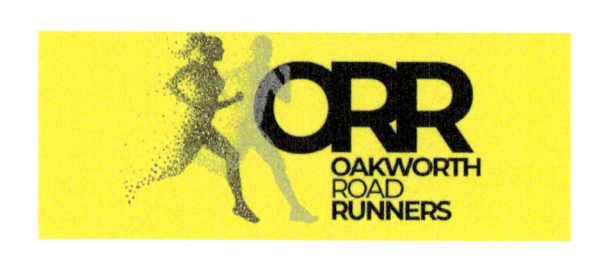

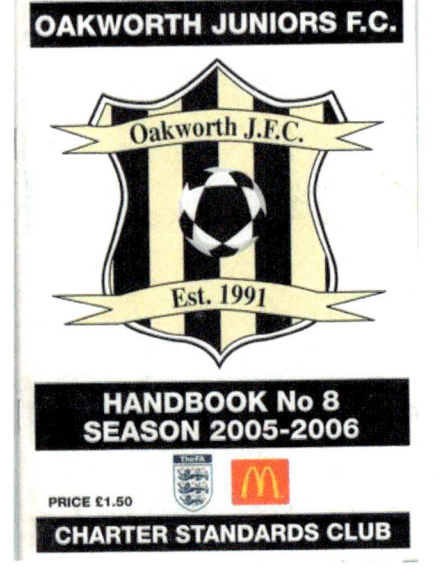

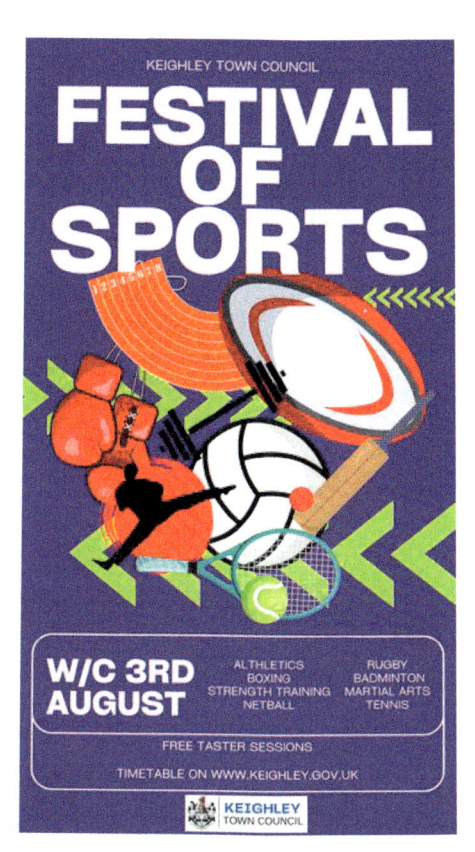

Promoting Sport in Keighley

2024 Flyer (left)

Hopefully the first of many Keighley Festivals of Sport. Clubs offering taster activities included; Riddlesden Tennis Club, Bradford, Keighley & Skipton Disability Athletics Club, Keighley Amateur Boxing Club, Keighley Kobras & Keighley Phoenix badminton clubs, Keighley & Craven Athletics Club, Strong Medicine Club strength training, England Netball, Keighley Albion RLFC and Beanland Taekwon-Do

Bradford, Keighley & Skipton Disability Athletics (below)

Steven Penny's **Keighley Kicks** promoted soccer in Keighley between 2011-18. John Dennis' **SportKeighley** promoted all sport in the town in the early 2000s.

Printed in Great Britain
by Amazon